Turn this book into a Scratch & Sniff Book

Order your FREE Scratch & Sniff labels
And pay only for Shipping & Handling

http://ScratchAndSniffTravel.com

WHAT DO YOU SMELL?

WHEN YOU GET YOUR SCRATCH & SNIFF CARD:

1. Peel the back off of the label.
2. Push the long edge into the binder with the Scratch & Sniff Stickers facing so that you can see them.
3. Each Smelly spot will match spices listed in the book.
4. Follow directions on the label.

**Enjoy and let me know what you think.
Please write a review on Amazon:**
http://Amazon.com/author/bruceoliver

Thanks for your purchase.

Bruce Oliver

"With Bruce Luxury Travel… the World is at your Feet"

Secrets of Cooking
Scratch & Sniff

Using Spices, Herbs & Salts (Illustrated)

with tidbits, stories and recipes

Be sure to check out my Travel & Food Series

A Sensational Travel & Food Resource Series™
SensationalTravelBooks.com

Traveling Coloring Books Series™
http://TravelingColoringBooks.com

Discover:

Cuba – Alaska – Vegas – Ireland – Hawaii

By Author: Bruce Oliver, Luxury Travel Host

Illustrator & Photographer: Bruce Oliver

Host of: BruceOliverTV.com – Smart TV Travel & Food Network

Axis Mundi Systems LLC dba Cruise with Bruce Enterprises

Copyright © 2019 by Bruce Oliver - Travel Advisor & TV Host

Published by Vegas New Wave Media

Be sure to use the Table of Contents (Page 11) and Index (Page 74) to find everything in the book. I hope that you use this book in your kitchen each time you cook and want to know what Spices, Herbs and Salts will enrich your culinary masterpiece.

The photograph used on the front and back covers, is courtesy of: Liv Otierk and her Amateur Travel Photography Blog located at: https://happywanderer15.wordpress.com. She said that:

"It is a picture of the spices for sale at the Grand Bazaar in Istanbul, Turkey. Again, the Bazaar is a great place to shop for tourists, but it's not super touristy. The vendors are friendly, and it's a great environment to walk around in. If you want more information look at the other post about spices"

Be sure to check out her blog for more great photos. Of course, I managed to get my face in the photo.

Printed in the United States of America.
ISBN-13 9781970029000
ISBN-10: 1970029005

Thanks for buying my book.

Bruce

"Take some time to Travel." ☁ smell the roses and

In Memorial to My Mom

0-1 *Photo by Bruce Oliver*

Elizabeth Oliver

Friend, Advisor, Traveling Companion

1927 to 2018

Acknowledgments

I have many people to thank for help in producing this book. I start with all of the hotels and institutions that contributed recipes including: Alice Boulez, Andrea Leyden, Anna Pellò, Barry Krushner, Carlotta Scarpa Olivi, Cody Thompson , Elisa Pepi, Emily Schmidt Liuzza, Gary Murphy, Jackie Collens, Jane Baldwin, Jeremy Heryet, Jessica Foss, Brittany Chavez, Jonathan Wood, Karen Candy, Laura E. Richeson, Lisa Dischinger, Melanie Wright, Meryl Press, Ms. Jerrol Golden, Nicholas Gandossi, Ondřej Kunc, Padraik McGillicuddy, Quentin Guiraud, Simone Dulies, Taylor Lee, Zuzana Šelová, Sandy Paugauguin. Their submissions help make this a valuable resource for travel, recipes and the ingredients that make them special.

I addition I'd like to thank my sister (Cathy Garvey) and my mom (Liz Oliver, Senior Editor in Chief) for being a sounding board. Their help caused me to make additions and changes as I went through the process to end up with what I present to you as the final product. I also thank many friends and family members that offered their advice from time to time.

Thanks to all those who helped me review content.

* Harry Schwartz.................... Celebrity Chef Harry
* Michael Cervin.................... Forbes magazine columnist................................
* Tony Pace........................... Las Vegas entertainer
* Gary Murphy .... Co-Owner, AmaWaterways River Cruise Line
* Kelly Bergin........................ President of OASIS ....
* Rick Robinson..................... Author and Educator
* Jim and Sandy Minneo........ Entrepreneurs

Foreword

"Bruce Oliver takes us on an olfactory tour of the world, where we not only learn about the herbs and spices we all use on a daily basis but also tantalizes us with recipes and wine pairings from some of the world's best hotels and their talented chefs. Unique, intriguing and a treat for all the senses, his Scent-Sational Travels: A Scratch and Sniff Experience is a one of a kind interactive book that makes you feel like you're in the thick of all things travel and food!" *~Michael Cervin, Forbes Travel Guides*

"Bruce Oliver's use of a directive of how to use this book is concise and so well laid out. I love his use of movie correlations. Brilliant Spice usage tables. This is one of the best layouts explaining where to use spices. The ethnic foods table was a surprise and my first thought was I can definitely use it every day; just perfect.

The use and history of the herbs gave me a better understanding of each. I especially appreciate the history. Well done on this. The Salt section is one of my favorites. I never realized the level of differences.

I was amazed at all the recipes from an eclectic level of places from around the world. Only Bruce Oliver could have brought this together with one of the most beautiful pictorial presentations. He made me feel like I was there.

This is one of the most comprehensive and well laid out reference guides I have ever seen. Bruce Oliver has created a masterpiece of information that appeals to all our senses. This book is the standard for the food and travel industry. Simply Genius. Congratulations." *Tony Pace, Vegas Headliner and Recording Artist*

"Bruce Oliver cooks as well as he cruises! Being a fan of eating my way around the globe, Bruce Oliver has put together the perfect travel guide for me." *Rick Robinson, award winning author*

"In these pages, Bruce Oliver makes travel a culinary escapade. Bruce's knowledge and culinary sense makes this a guide for those hungry for travel and great food and wine." *Chef Harry Schwartz Author, Columnist, Show Host, Media Chef, Culinary Creator*

"Bruce Oliver did a nice job putting together this scratch and sniff travel and food book. What a unique idea! I love the information that is available for booking hotels and cruises. And I'll be using the recipes as well." *Kelly Bergin, President, Palm Coast Travel*

"In a word. Simply outstanding!! I have read several recipes now and I am getting so hungry. I love the scratch and sniff idea too!!!" *Jeff Froehlich, Director of Sales & Marketing, OPUS Vancouver*

"I found myself reading the book at work - caught myself and got back to work. Congratulations." *Gary Murphy, Co-Owner, AmaWaterways River Cruises*

"Bruce Oliver's Scent-Sational experience book looks fabulous." *Alice Boulez, Associate Director of Sales & Marketing, Hôtel du Louve Paris*

"What a novel idea: 'scratch and sniff travel and food'. We loved learning how executive chefs use spices, herbs and salts while they cook. The historical information, tidbits and quotes also makes the book an interesting read. It's a great resource for travelers and non-travelers alike; you can smell the ingredients before you use them. We plan to keep the book in our kitchen as a resource while cooking new and old dishes." *James and Sandy Minneo, Entrepreneurs*

Table of Illustrations

Traveling Is Good For Your Health!

As a youth, I listened to my elders say, over and over,

0-1 Illustration by Bruce Oliver

that the one thing they wish they had done more often was take longer vacations when they had their young families. Seldom did someone say I wish I had worked more. Couples who wait until retirement to travel may have lost their opportunity to travel while they were together or in good health. Now, one woman said, he's passed and it's too late. Another said, "When we were young, we thought that we'd be healthy forever. But now I must go for dialysis and it's too late! (Not really, many cruise lines can accommodate people on dialysis.)

My father relayed the same information to me as his health was failing just before his death. The prior year, for the first time in his life, he and mom went with my brother, sister, her son, my aunt and uncle and I on a two-week vacation to Edinburg, Scotland and

0-3 Photo by Bruce Oliver

0-2 Illustration by Bruce Oliver

London, England. He said that he wished he had more time to go again but it was too late for him, "not for you" he said, "Now I understand why you always travel." People nearing the end of life always say they wish that they took more time to "smell the roses".

I love everything about travel. Early in life I always made time to go somewhere new. Maybe it was because I belonged to a Scout Troop that always took us on vacations to Washington,

0-4 Photo by Bruce Oliver

D.C., World's Fairs in Montreal and New York City or destinations that the average boy would never visit. As an

Eagle Scout, I was awarded a 30-day bus trip across the United States to hike for twelve days at Philmont National Boy Scout Reservation in Cimarron, NM. Today, I plan and use my vacations because I tend to be a workaholic. I plan

0-5 Photo by Bruce Oliver

a two-week vacation at least once per year and each quarter I have weekend trips to look forward to. This is especially important when things get difficult. Life is a sine wave with ups and downs. When the down periods come, I always say, but I'm going on a cruise in a few weeks. Knowing this helps me cope with the downs and I am more productive.

0-6 Illustration by Bruce Oliver

As a matter of fact, productivity experts have discovered that the longer it is between vacations: "Fatigue

0-7 Illustration by Bruce Oliver

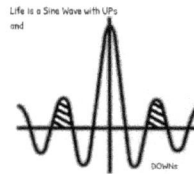

sets in, rigidity applies, and all creativity and innovation are lost — both of which need time away for other activities to increase the probability of new ideas," said Lotte Bailyn, an MIT researcher and author of the book "Breaking the Mold: Redesigning Work for Productive and Satisfying Lives. (Bailyn, 2006)" "Unhealthy overwork costs company's money for healthcare and creates stressful and unrewarding lives, both of which detract from the good work they are supposed to be furthering."

Everything that I've read says the same thing. The more and longer vacations that you take, the more productive you will be when you get back to work. I feel best coming back from a two-week vacation (I don't mean visiting relatives to paint their house either.) It usually takes me 3-4 days to begin to relax and the balance of the vacation is full of rest and relaxation. I've gotten to the point that the only time I say I'm on vacation is when I leave the country and get away from the phone which I answer 24/7 and my normal regiment.

According to Ellen Galinsky, President of Families and Work Institute, the longer your vacation, the less stress you'll feel. People's stress levels dropped significantly when they took over 6-days and more as they approached 13 or more consecutive days away from work and their regular routine life. Families participating in these vacations tend to be less depressed and form tighter bonds with other family members (Ellen Galinski,

0-8 Illustration by Bruce Oliver

2014). It's true, my siblings and I often talk about the time we spent camping each summer at Lake Ossipee in New Hampshire or at Clinton Beach in Connecticut.

Galinski says: "Knowing that skipping vacation stifles creativity, creates health problems, leads to stress, depression, and less-than-ideal home lives, it seems as if companies would make vacation enforcement a priority. But with a few exceptions, the experts say that is not happening. Vacation skipping is a topic that's often swept under the keyboard."

Both women and men alike benefit by taking vacations. After their study, Gump, PhD, MPH, and; Matthews, PhD at the American Psychosomatic Society, concluded: "The frequency of annual vacations by middle-aged men at high risk for coronary heart disease (CHD) is associated with a reduced risk of all-cause mortality and, more specifically, mortality attributed to CHD. **Vacationing may be good for your health.**" (Gump & Matthews, 2000)

CONTENTS

Cooking With
Fine Herbs & Spices

When I started this project, I *did not* want to create just *one more ho-hum* book that just lists spices and herbs from around the world. I wanted to bring that world to you! I wanted something different, something to Spice up your Life! Something with interaction, fun to share to provide a healthful tasty experience.

I wanted something different than just another run of the mill recipe book. It is to be informative, interesting, useful and filled with tidbits you might not know and food trivia and history that I wanted to share.

Plus…. I wanted you to learn that there are many fines spices that change the entire flavor of even the simplest meal. Don't you love a great kitchen full of aromatics! This book is how to become a super cook by using the finest spices and seasonings properly.

I worked to create an interesting book with recipes, food trivia and tidbits of
… *"ahhaa, I didn't know that" ….!*

For recipes from the World's Best Cruise Lines and Hotels, check out my Scratch and Sniff Travel Series available on my website at the back of the book.

*Register to win an All-Inclusive Holiday with airfare at: http://Win.CruiseWithBruce.com to receive a **DISCOUNT CODE**. Check that you allow email contact.*

*The code is good for up to a 10 % on group travel, books, spices & salts, Scratch and Sniff Greeting Cards, etc. Then **follow me** on **Facebook** and **Twitter** for more information.*

Using Spices and Herbs

How

Use this book to determine the one or two spices and herbs that you wish to add to your dish. Moisture destroys the strength of the herbs and spices causing them to spoil. So always use a dry spoon to add small portions of the spices and herbs to complement the natural flavor of the dish and not so much that it masks or over-powers the natural taste of the ingredients.

Crush fresh leafy herbs such as oregano, thyme or basil before using them to release their flavor. If they are dry you may want to use them with butter, oil or water.

When

Always add herbs like fresh dill and parsley to your dish near the end of cooking cycle. Adding them too early causes the herb to lose their aroma and taste. Never add them at the beginning of a cooking cycle. Spices like paprika don't change unless they are used in dishes cooked over eight hours. Salt does not change in taste regardless of how long you cook your meal.

When adding ground spices and herbs to the pot earlier their flavors are released immediately. Add them mid-way to the end of a cooking cycle when cooking dishes such as stews or spaghetti sauces that simmer for a day. This way the flavor doesn't dissipate.

Bay leaves and whole spices take longer to release their flavor than ground or leaf form. They are best used for dishes that take longer to cook. When "slow cooking" always cook your dish at a lower temperature. You should always remove the leaves prior to serving the meal. The rule of thumb is when you add and simmer it becomes part of the dish. When you add at the end you get bursts of it while eating.

Adding spices and herbs to fruits, fruit juices or, salad dressings, as well as other uncooked foods should be done long enough in advance of serving them to allow the flavors to bond with each other. Marinades help break down tough meats like London broil and enhance the flavor of meat and fish by placing it in a plastic bag and placed in the refrigerator overnight (turn the bag over occasionally get the full effect).

Amount

Start with ½ teaspoon of spice servings for any dish 4-6 people. When adding herbs use ½ teaspoon for powder and 1-1/2 teaspoon for dried or chopped herbs. Taste the dish and adjust as necessary. Use less cayenne and garlic powder in the beginning then add more to taste.

Adding spices and herbs is a matter of taste. The correct amount comes down to the type of food and the strength and pungency of the spice or herb in question. Begin using a little, then taste and add more if the dish still needs it. Begin using the ingredients suggested in this book or from a tried and true family recipe. Then add a little more at a time until the food has a flavor that you appreciate. If a dish becomes too salty then you may want to dilute it with water. The cooler a dish is the less we taste the spices and herbs that have been added.

> *A good tasting vanilla ice cream is harder to make than any other flavor!* Mistakes while making it are covered by adding chocolate or other flavors!

Spice Usage Tips*

	Appetizers	Soups	Eggs & Cheese	Meats	Fish & Seafood	Salads	Sauces & Relishes	Vegetables	Breads & Desserts
Allspice	Meatballs	Split Pea Oyster Stew Bean		Ham Beef Stew Meat Loaf Jerk Chicken	Spiced Shrimp Poached Fish	Pickled Beets	Catsup Chili Sauce	Sweet Potatoes, Asparagus, Beets Broccoli, Cabbage, Peas, Carrots, Zucchini, Winter Squash	Cookies, Cakes, Pies Coffee Cakes, Pudding Baked Custard, Fruit Hot Spiced Beverages
Basil	Seafood Cocktail Tomato Juice Cheese Spreads	Minestrone Beef, Tomato Vegetable, Chicken	Cheese Soufflé Scrambled Eggs Omelets, Quiche Deviled Eggs	Beef Stew Roast & Fried Chicken Italian Foods Hamburgers, Roasts	Baked & Poached Fish Tuna & Salmon Loaf	Chicken Tuna Seafood Vegetable	Spaghetti Cheese Sauce Barbeque Sauce Marinara Sauce	Asparagus, Beets, Broccoli, Carrots, Corn, Peas, Cabbage, Green Beans, Potatoes, Tomatoes, Winter Squash, Zucchini	Herb Bread Breadsticks Focaccia
Bay		Bean Vegetable Beef Chicken		Stews Corned Beef Pot Roast	Poached Fish Spiced Shrimp, Boiled Shrimp	Aspic	Tomato Sauce Spaghetti Sauce Barbeque Sauce	Potatoes	
Caraway Seed	Cheese Spread	Borscht Potato	Cottage Cheese	Sauerbraten Stews		Coleslaw Pickled Beets		Cabbage, Carrots, Sauerkraut	Cookies Rye Bread

Spice	Appetizers	Soups	Eggs & Cheese	Meats	Fish & Seafood	Salads	Sauces & Relishes	Vegetables	Breads & Desserts
Celery Seed	Meatballs, Dips Cheese Spreads Seafood Cocktail Tomato Juice	Vegetable Tomato	Cottage Cheese Deviled Eggs	Stews, Pot Roasts Meatloaf	Baked Fish	Shrimp, Tuna Potato Salad Dressing Coleslaw	Barbeque Sauce Cocktail Sauce	Potatoes, Cauliflower, Green Beans, Peas, Tomatoes	Biscuits Muffins
Chili Powder	Cheese Spreads Shrimp Cocktail Nachos Salsa	Chili, Beef, Bean, Vegetable Gazpacho	Omelets Deviled Eggs	Fajitas Stews, Hamburgers Roast & Fried Chicken Tacos		Bean Taco	Taco Sauce Barbeque Sauce Tomato Sauce	Corn, Cauliflower, Green Beans, Peas, Tomatoes	
	Appetizers	Soups	Eggs & Cheese	Meats	Fish & Seafood	Salads	Sauces & Relishes	Vegetables	Breads & Desserts
Cinnamon	Fruit Cocktail	Split Pea Fruit	Cottage Cheese Dessert Omelet	Stews Braised Meats Chicken Stuffing Ham		Fruit	Chutney, Catsup Mole Sauce Fruit Sauce, Relishes Chocolate Sauce	Beets, Carrots, Corn, Winter Squash, Sweet Potatoes	Coffee Cakes, Pies, Fruit, Muffins, Yeast Breads, Cakes, Cookies, Puddings, Hot Spiced Beverages
Cloves	Fruit Cocktail Cranberry Juice Apple Cider	Split Pea	Eggnog Fruit Omelet	Ham, Braised Meats Corned Beef Roast Chicken	Poached Fish Spiced Shrimp	Pickled Beets	Chutney Relishes	Beets, Carrots, Cabbage, Winter Squash, Sweet Potato	Coffee Cake, Cake Cookies, Pies Pudding, Fruit Hot Spiced Beverages
Cumin	Nachos Meatballs Guacamole	Chili Vegetable Beef	Scrambled Eggs Omelets, Quiche	Roast Beef Pork Chicken	Fish Tacos	Avocado Marinated Vegetables Bean	Barbeque Sauce Mexican Sauce	Tomatoes, Green Beans Corn Zucchini	

		Gazpacho		Mexican Dishes			Vegetable Sauce	
Curry Powder	Shrimp & Seafood Cocktails Dips Spreads	Chicken Beef Seafood	Deviled Eggs Scrambled Eggs Egg Salad	Curries Chicken, Beef, Veal, Lamb, Roasts Stews	Shrimp Creamed Tuna or Salmon	Marinated Vegetable Chicken Seafood	Cream Sauce Chutney	Broccoli, Cabbage, Carrots, Cauliflower, Corn, Green Beans, Peas, Potatoes, Zucchini
Dill weed	Dips Spreads Fish & Seafood Cocktails	Chicken Split Pea Potato Chowders	Deviled, Scrambled & Creamed Eggs, Quiche, Soufflés, Omelets, Cottage Cheese	Lamb, Veal & Pork Roasts Chicken Casseroles Hamburgers	Tuna or Salmon Loaf Seafood Casseroles Baked & Broiled Fish	Chicken, Shrimp, Vegetable Potato, Cucumber Coleslaw	Cheese Sauce Cream Sauce Relishes	Asparagus, Beets, Green Beans, Broccoli, Cabbage, Potatoes, Carrots, Cauliflower, Corn, Peas, Tomatoes, Zucchini

* NOTE: This table is being used with compliments of ACH Foods, Inc.

	Appetizers	Soups	Eggs & Cheese	Meats	Fish & Seafood	Salads	Sauces & Relishes	Vegetables	Breads & Desserts
Garlic	Dips Spreads	Chicken Vegetable	Omelets	Roast Chicken Burgers Italian, Mexican or Asian Dishes	Baked Fish Shrimp Scampi	Vegetable Potato Salad Dressings	Italian-Style Sauces Barbeque Sauce	Mashed or Roasted Potatoes, Tomatoes, Zucchini	Breadsticks Focaccia French Bread
Ginger	Broiled Grapefruit	Split Pea Bean Fruit		Marinades Ham, Braised Meats Stir-Fry	Marinades	Fruit Chicken	Chutney Relishes Fruit	Asparagus, Beets, Carrots, Winter Squash, Sweet Potatoes, Stir-fried Vegetables	Coffee Cakes Gingerbread Cake, Fruit Cookies
Marjoram	Dips Spreads	Vegetable, Beef Chicken, Onion, Seafood, Fish Tomato	Scrambled Eggs Quiche, Soufflé Omelet	Stews, Roast & Fried Chicken, Meat Loaf Meat Balls, Roasts	Baked & Broiled Fish	Marinated Vegetable Chicken	Italian Sauce Tomato Sauce Cream Sauce	Asparagus, Broccoli, Cabbage, Carrots, Cauliflower, Corn, Green Beans, Peas, Potatoes, Tomatoes, Squash	
Mustard	Dips Meat Spreads Meatballs Pretzels	Chili	Omelets Quiche Deviled Eggs Egg Salad	Sausage Pork Ham Chicken	Baked & Broiled Fish	Vegetable Potato Coleslaw Salad Dressings	Honey Mustard Barbeque Marinades	Baked Beans Marinated Vegetables Pickles	
Nutmeg	Fruit Cocktail	Split Pea Chowders	Quiche Fruit Omelet Eggnog	Veal, Ham Meat Loaf Sausage		Chicken Fruit	Cream Sauce Dessert Sauces Chocolate Sauce	Asparagus, Beets, Broccoli, Cabbage, Potatoes, Carrots, Cauliflower, Green Beans, Peas, Squash, Sweet Potatoes	Muffins, Custard, Coffee Cakes, Cookies Pudding, Fruit, Pies

	Appetizers	Soups	Eggs & Cheese	Meats	Fish & Seafood	Salads	Sauces & Relishes	Vegetables	Breads & Desserts
Oregano	Dips Spreads Meatballs Tomato Juice	Minestrone Tomato, Beef Vegetable, Bean	Soufflés, Quiche Omelets Scrambled & Deviled Eggs	Roast & Fried Chicken Meat Loaf Roasts, Stews Braised Meats	Baked & Broiled Fish Shrimp	Bean Vegetable Potato Salad Dressings	Italian-Style Sauce Spaghetti Sauce Tomato Sauce Barbeque Sauce	Asparagus, Broccoli, Corn, Green Beans, Peas, Roasted Potatoes, Tomatoes, Zucchini	Muffins Biscuits Herb Breads
Rosemary	Meatballs	Chicken Pea	Soufflés Scrambled Eggs	Roast Lamb Veal Chicken Pork Roasts	Broiled & Poached Fish	Tomatoes Salad Dressings Cucumber		Gravy	Corn, Green Beans, Peas, Roasted Potatoes, Tomatoes, Zucchini
Sage	Cheese Spreads Meatballs	Chicken Pea Tomato	Soufflés Quiche, Omelets Creamed & Scrambled Eggs	Chicken & Pork Dishes Stuffing Sausage	Stuffed Fish Baked Fish Broiled Fish	Salad Dressings	Poultry Gravy	Green Beans, Brussels Sprouts, Peas, Zucchini	Muffins Biscuits
Tarragon	Cheese Spreads Seafood Cocktail Pate Tomato Juice	Chicken Vegetable Tomato	Omelets, Soufflés, Quiche Deviled & Creamed Eggs	Chicken & Pork Dishes Roast Pork, Veal, Lamb & Chicken	Broiled & Poached Fish Seafood	Tomatoes Cucumber Vegetable Salad Dressings	Hollandaise Poultry Gravy Béarnaise	Broccoli, Carrots, Cauliflower, Green Beans, Peas, Potatoes, Tomatoes, Zucchini	
Thyme	Cheese Spreads Dips Pate Seafood Cocktails	Vegetable, Pea Beef, Chicken Tomato, Bean Minestrone	Soufflés, Omelets Scrambled Eggs Cottage Cheese Quiche	Baked & Fried Chicken Braised Meats, Roasts, Pork Chops Stuffing	Baked & Broiled Fish Seafood	Salad Dressings Potato & Vegetable Salads, Tomatoes, Cucumbers	Hollandaise Gravy Tomato Sauce	Asparagus, Broccoli, Carrots, Cauliflower, Corn, Green Beans, Peas, Potatoes, Tomatoes, Zucchini, Brussels Sprouts, Onions	Herb Bread

* NOTE: This table is being used with the compliments of ACH Foods, Inc.

Spices used for Ethnic Foods

Column numbers corresponding with table below:

1 – Asian (a) (In addition stock: Soy sauce and/or Tamari, Rice Vinegar, Fish Sauce, Chili Sauce, Oyster Sauce, Coconut Milk, Miso Paste, Rice Wine, and Lime)

2 – Eastern European (e)   3 – French (f)

4 – Italian (i)   5 – Mediterranean (m)

6 – Mexican (x)   7 – Moroccan (x) (+ Almonds, Olive Oil)

8 – Spanish (s)   9 – Baking (b)

10 – Holiday Cooking & Baking (h)

	1	2	3	4	5	6	7	8	9	10
Allspice					m				b	h
Anise					m		x		b	
Annatto					m					
Apple Mint										
Basil				i	m					
Bay Leaves			f	i	m		x	s		
Bergamot										
Borage										
Caledula										
Caraway					m					
Cayenne Pepper							x			
Chamomile										
Cardamon			f		m				b	
Chervil					m					
Chili Pepper				i	m	x		s		
Chive			f		m					
Cilantro	a				m		x			
Cinnamon					m		x	m	b	h
Cloves					m		x		b	h
Coriander					m	x				
Cumin					m	x	x	m		
Curry	a									
Dill										
Fennel			f	i	m		x			
Fenugreek					m		x			
French Sorrel										
Garlic			f		m	x		s		
Ginger	a				m		x		b	

	1	2	3	4	5	6	7	8	9	10
Horehound										
Horseradish										
Hyssop										
Juniper Berry		e			m					
Lavender										
Lemon Balm										
Lemon Verbena							x			
Lovage										
Mace		e			m		x		b	
Marjoram		e	f		m					
Mint		e			m		x			
Mustard		e								
Nutmeg		e	f		m		x		b	
Onion			f		m		x			
Oregano				i	m	x	x	s		
Orris Root										
Paprika		e			m		x			h
Parsley		e	f		m		x	s		
Pepper		e	f		m		x		b	
Poppy Seeds		e							b	
Red Pepper	a						x			
Rosemary			f	i	m			s		
Saffron			f		m		x	s		
Sage			f	i	m		x			h
Salad Burnet										
Savory					m					h
Sesame Seed	a						x		b	
Sweet Woodruff										
Tarragon			f		m					
Thyme			f	i	m		x			
Turmeric					m		x			
Vanilla									b	

The Difference Herbs vs. Spices

NOTE: Most the spices that we use today are from the Eastern Hemisphere and tropical destinations like South East Asia, India and the Mediterranean.

Did you know that a different parts of the same plant can be used as an herb or a spice?

- Leafy green parts are usually used as an herb.
- Spices are usually seeds, flowers, root stems or the bark.

Notes

Spices: Use & History

Allspice or pimento

Allspice or pimento is the little round berry of an evergreen tree common in the West Indies. It contains about 4% of an aromatic oil. The warm sweet flavor of Allspice lends itself to a wide variety of savory and sweet foods. Allspice may be substituted for cloves. Food producers use it in ketchup, pickles, and sausages. The Jamaicans use Allspice in curries, jerk seasoning, soups, and stews. It also is used in cakes, cookies, pickling spice, pies, spiced and tea mixes. Try mixing 1/4 teaspoon ground Allspice with a couple pounds of ground beef to add flavor to meatloaf and hamburgers. Or, add 1 teaspoon of ground Allspice to angel food or white cake mix for a unique spicy flavor. For a seasoning blend add a few Whole Allspice to your pepper grinder, along with a mixture of black, white, and green peppercorns. For an fascinating spiciness, add the whole Allspice cracked berries to marinades for simmering beef stew, chicken, hearty bean soups, pork, or pot roasts. Add the sweet, warm flavor of ground Allspice to applesauce, fruit compotes, as well as oatmeal. Add a touch of Allspice (ground up) to barbecue carrots, cooked winter squash and tomato sauces.

History: Christopher Columbus discovered Allspice in the Caribbean. Although he was seeking pepper, he had never actually seen real pepper and he thought Allspice was it. He brought it back to Spain, where it got the name "pimienta," which is Spanish for pepper. Its Anglicized name, pimento, is occasionally used in the spice trade today. Before World War II, Allspice was more widely used than it is nowadays. During the war, many trees producing Allspice were cut, and production never fully recovered. Folklore suggests that Allspice provides relief for digestive problems.

Cayenne Pepper

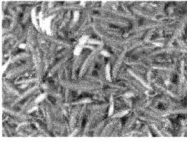

Made from a small, spicy red pepper, this is the foundation of many bottled hot sauces. It has little aroma, but it is extremely hot to taste. Used frequently in Cajun, Asia, the Americas, and the Middle East and Indian recipes. Cayenne Pepper comes from India. Try adding Cayenne Pepper to salsa, avocado dip, taco, and enchilada sauces for extra zesty flavor. You can heat up a barbecue sauce or meat marinade with a shake of Cayenne Pepper. Spice up your tartar sauce or vegetable dips and dressings with a pinch of Cayenne Pepper. You can make South-of-the-Border omelets with tomatoes, onions, peppers, and a pinch of Cayenne Pepper added to the eggs.

History: One of Columbus' passengers, de Cuneo, wrote how the Native Americans ate pepper-like fruit like we eat apples. Cayenne Peppers were grown for thousands of years in the West Indies and Central and South America. Spanish explorers looking for black pepper misnamed them as pepper, and introduced them to the rest of the world.

Chili Powder

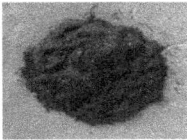

This is typically made from a blend of dried chilies, chili peppers, coriander, oregano, cumin, and garlic powder. Chili Powder mixtures can vary from mild to extremely spicy. It is not necessarily hot, but may have a mild flavor if made with a chili pepper of a less pungent variety. Use small amounts of the hot variety of this spice and taste the food before adding more. Chili Powders can often be used in sodium-free cooking, since many are made without salt. Chili powder provides the hot flavor of Cajun, Creole, Mexican, Indian, Thai and Szechuan, cooking. Manufacturers use chili powder in processed Mexican food. Use it to make a dip to complement fruit and vegetable sticks or with pork and beans, and sausages. Chili Powder is used in Mexican and Southwestern-type cooking. It's a prominent ingredient of chili con carne, and is also used in cheese dishes, to season eggs, shellfish, and stews.

Use the flakes of crushed red chili to sprinkle on pizzas, to spice up pastas with stir-fries. It also is used in barbecue sauce as well as casseroles, chili, meats, Spanish rice, and salads. As it is cooked the flavor increases. It is a biting condiment. When you add chili pepper (ground) and salt to hot oil and sauté blanched almonds to a golden color you can create a spicy snack. Make scrambled eggs or an omelet with bacon, cheese, onion and a dash of chili pepper to create a different dish. Try adding it to barbecue sauce and to baste and/or marinate steaks for the grill.

History: Chili Powder was invented in the American Southwest during the 19th century. It was an American attempt to create a mixture of chili peppers and other herbs like those used by the Aztecs in Mexico. Capsicum peppers are native to Mexico, Central America, the West Indies, and parts of South America. The Spanish discovered the pods in the New World and brought them back to Europe. Before the arrival of Spaniards, Indians in Peru and Guatemala used capsicum medicinally to treat stomach and other ailments.

Cilantro AKA Coriander

Cilantro is the leaf of the young coriander plant. Cilantro's taste is a fragrant mix of parsley and citrus. is traditionally used in Middle Eastern, Mexican, and Asian cooking. Before it is used, Cilantro should be crushed, either by hand or with a mortar and pestle. Cilantro is a perfect addition to Mexican dishes; add Cilantro to salsas and bean dips. Mix crushed Cilantro into sour cream as a topping for chili, tacos, or enchiladas. Sprinkle Cilantro over stir-fried vegetables for color and Asian flavor. Add Cilantro to sesame-ginger dressing for Chinese chicken salad.

History: Cilantro is currently grown in California. The young Coriander leaves were first used over 7000 years ago. It is mentioned in early Sanskrit writings dating from about 1500 BC. The Romans spread it throughout Europe, and it was one of the first spices to arrive in America.

Cinnamon

Cinnamon Sticks

Cinnamon is the dried bark of various laurel trees that grow in Ceylon. The best cinnamon sticks are dry and very thin with the outer and inner coats of the bark removed. Ground Cinnamon is perhaps the most common baking spice. This warm, aromatic spice has a reddish-brown color and a bittersweet flavor. Great for baking as well as adding an earthiness to stews, chilies, and curries. Possibly most the common baking spice, Cinnamon is used in cakes, cookies, and desserts throughout the world. Cinnamon is also used in savory chicken and lamb dishes from the Middle East. Cinnamon's sweet-spicy flavor enhances the taste of fruits and vegetables. In American cooking, Cinnamon is often paired with apples and used in other fruit and cereal dishes. When used in an apple pie it mellows the tart taste of some apples. Stick Cinnamon is used in pickling and for flavoring hot beverages. For a fragrant pilaf, cook rice in Cinnamon flavored broth and stir in chopped dried fruit and toasted nuts. Cinnamon is a perfect partner for chocolate; use it in any chocolate dessert or drink.

Ground Cinnamon should not be added to boiling liquids; the liquid may become stringy and the Cinnamon will lose flavor.

History: Most people love the smell of cinnamon. Popular since ancient times the Egyptians discovered and imported in 2000 BC. The Romans believed Cinnamon was sacred and considered it to be a gift fitting for the gods. It has been written that Nero burned a year's supply of the spice at the funeral for his wife. Finding Cinnamon was a primary motive of world exploration in the 15th and 16th centuries and was traded along the spice route.

Cloves

Cloves are the brown, dried, rich, unopened flower buds of an evergreen tree in the myrtle family. They grow in Africa, the East Indies and South America, ranking in value in the order named. The best cloves contain as much as 16% of a volatile oil to which their flavor is due. Ground cloves have sometimes a portion of this oil pressed out, with pimento or allspice added, which latter is much less costly. Cloves are best when large, plump, bright in tint, and full of oil, which exudes on pressure with the finger nail. A little goes a long way so use it sparingly. This sweet, rich spice is a staple in holiday baking, especially gingersnaps, gingerbread, spice cookies, cakes, applesauce, muffins, and other sweets. A closely guarded secret, many people use it in barbecue and cocktail sauces. Maple syrup blended with Ground Cloves can be drizzle over cooked sweet potatoes and winter squash. Add a couple whole Cloves (remove before serving) to bean and split pea soups.

> The name Cloves comes from the French word "clou" meaning nail.

History: Cloves have been used for thousands of years and originally grew in the Molucca Islands, now a part of Indonesia. Natives on the islands planted a Clove tree for each child born believing that the fate of the tree was linked to the fate of that child. The Chinese even put few Cloves in their mouths to sweeten their breath before meeting with the emperor. In 1816 Cloves were so valuable that the Dutch fought the islanders on Molucca to secure rights to the profitable Clove business even burning the clove trees to raise prices.

Cumin

An aromatic, mellow spice, ground from a small seed. Ground Cumin is stronger than whole seeds.

The Cumin flavor is accentuated by toasting. Delicious in Middle Eastern and Indian cooking, especially curries. Cumin is frequently used in Mexican dishes such as chili con carne and hot tamales. Or, add Cumin to chili, spicy meat stews, barbecue marinades, and sauces. For a change of pace, try ground Cumin added to tangy lime or lemon-based marinades for chicken, turkey, lamb, and pork. For a south-of-the-border taste, stir Cumin that has been toasted into corn muffin batter. Heat garlic and Cumin in olive oil the drizzle it over potatoes or cooked vegetables.

History: The increasing popularity of Mexican influenced foods is boosting the sale of Cumin. Currently cumin is grown in many places, as it is rather easy to grow and adapts well to many climates. In ancient times Cumin was native to the shores of the Mediterranean Sea and Egypt. A favorite of the Romans and mentioned in the Old Testament cumin was used in Europe and Britain during medieval times. Today it isn't as popular as it was back then.

Curry Powder

Curry Powder is made of up to 20 spices including coriander, cumin, and turmeric are in this popular Indian blend. The Madras variety has more heat. This compound of spices, etc., is much used in India and other hot countries, as an appetizer and stimulant to digestion. Curry is used in dips to complement fruit and vegetable sticks, blend Curry Powder with yogurt or sour cream marmalade, and thyme to make the dip. Try adding Curry Powder to deviled eggs and egg salads. You can easily make an East Indian marinade for chicken or lamb with Curry Powder, yogurt, lime or lemon juice, and garlic.

Ginger

Fresh Ginger Root

Ginger is the root-stalk of a plant which grows in Jamaica and other warm countries. The odor of ginger is due to an essential oil; its pungency to a peculiar resin. The best comes with the skin scraped off and ground. Ground ginger has a more intense and astringent taste than fresh ginger. Keep it on hand for baking. Ginger is also used on cruise ships to settle passenger's stomachs when experiencing rough seas.

In the 19th century it was popular to keep a shaker of Ginger on the counter in English pubs so the patrons could shake some into their drinks. *This practice was the origin of ginger ale.*

History: Ginger originated in the tropical rainforest in Southern Asia. Ginger was exported to Europe via India in the first century AD because of the lucrative spice trade and was used extensively by the Romans. It's believed that the longer the root, the longer the plant has grown in the area. It was one of the important spices that led to the opening of the spice trade routes by Marco Polo.

Mustard

Black Mustard Seed

Two large shrubs produce the Mustard Seed. White and brown mustard grow in Asia. The shrubs have bright yellow flowers with small round seeds; white mustard is less pungent than brown. This is the flour of the black or white mustard seed. The black seed contains most volatile oil, is more pungent, and differs from the white in chemical composition. The two are blended in various proportions. Wheat flour is often added, with a little turmeric to bring up the color. Mustard seed contains over 30% of a fixed oil, and a portion of this is often extracted. This practice is considered beneficial rather than fraudulent. Mustard Seed's hot and spicy flavor enhances fish, fowl, meats, salad dressings, and sauces. Whole seeds may be used when pickling or in boiling cabbage and sauerkraut or similar vegetables. Brown seeds are an important flavoring in Indian dishes. Mustard in the powdered form emits no aroma when dry, and has a hot flavor when it is mixed with water. To begin take your mustard powder and mix it with water to form a paste; within 10 minutes the mustard flavor will develop. The flavor of mustard doesn't increase but fades with time unlike other pungent spices. Use in foods needing flavor highlights. Mustard helps blend vinegar and oil adding a spicy taste when making salad dressings.

History: Mustard powder was invented by Mrs. Clements of Durham, England, who made a fortune selling the dry, pale-yellow mustard flour. The ancient Romans and Greeks used mustard as a flavoring and medicine. By 800 AD, the French were using Mustard as an enhancement for drab meals and salted meats. It was one of the spices taken on Spanish explorations during the 1400s.

Nutmeg & Mace

Nutmeg is the seed of *Myristica Fragrans*, an evergreen tree native to the Molucca Islands in the East Indies. Interestingly, the tree produces both Nutmeg and mace, and grows up to 60 feet tall. Although the tree takes seven years to bear fruit, it may produce until the 90th year. Both spices come from the tree's fruit, which splits into a scarlet red outer membrane, mace, and an inner brown seed called Nutmeg. Nutmeg's a warm, delicate spice often used by bakers. Also, a common addition to béchamel sauce, baked winter squash and spinach dishes. Good nutmegs are not worm eaten and feel heavy. They contain about 8% of volatile oil, and 25% of fixed oil, which exudes under indentation or pressure with the finger nail. Most people buy whole nutmegs and the ground article has only a limited sale. Mace is the arillus or coating of the nutmeg, and is also sold whole or unground. Nutmeg is a mild baking spice and is used in sausages, meats, soups, and preserves. Nutmeg is commonly added to eggnog, puddings, and fruit pies. It is popular in The Netherlands and Italy, where it is used in vegetables, puddings, and stews. Nutmeg is more pungent and sweeter than mace. The sweet but slightly bitter flavor of Nutmeg adds character to vegetables. A little goes a long way so try 1/8 teaspoon per 4 servings to start. Just sprinkle it lightly over veal, fish, or chicken for a surprising snap. Use as a topping for custard, eggnog and whipped cream. Ground Nutmeg is an great baking spice and is used in cakes, cookies, fruit pies, muffins, and sweet breads.

History

Until the mid-19th century the Banda Islands (AKA the 'Spice Islands') was the only place on earth that grew the trees producing the seed. The Portuguese discovered Nutmeg trees in the Molucca Islands, and controlled the Mace and Nutmeg trade until 1602 when the Dutch became the best source of the spice. A Dutch government official had the Moluccan islanders plant more Mace trees and fewer Nutmeg trees because he didn't realize that both spices came from one tree. In the 1800s, production of Nutmeg spread to the West Indies, Trinidad, and Grenada with the British. Nutmeg also grows in Grenada and Indonesia. In the first century, Pliny, a Roman philosopher wrote about Nutmeg and mace. Indian Vedic literature recommended Nutmeg for bad breath, fever and headaches. Arabian writing mentions its use as an aphrodisiac and stomach medicine. Middle Eastern traders brought Nutmeg and mace to Southern Europe in the sixth century and by the twelfth century both were well-known from Italy to Denmark.

Paprika

Paprika is a spice which comes from a mild red pepper in the family Capsicum annum. Paprika is sweet red pepper pods ground up into a powder, there are two varieties: sweet and hot. (If the type is not indicated on the bottle, it's most likely sweet.) It is a brilliant red powder and often used as a garnish. The best Paprika is from Hungary, used as the main flavor in Hungarian cooking, including dishes such as Goulash and Chicken Paprikash. In the United States, it is often used as a garnish on stuffed eggs, fish, and cheese and vegetable casseroles. Spanish Paprika flavors shellfish, rice, and sausage dishes. In Morocco, Paprika is used in tomato dishes and salads. Use the spice to season meat, seafood, and vegetables. Paprika is useful as a simple garnish for almost any savory dish like deviled eggs. Combine it with butter, margarine, or oil for a quick baste for fish or poultry. This is especially good on roast turkey. Paprika can be mixed with bread crumbs before sprinkling them over casseroles or vegetables.

History: Paprika, as a member of the capsicum family, is indigenous to the Western Hemisphere. The pepper is grown widely and takes on a slightly different flavor depending on local soil and climatic conditions.

Peppercorns

(Black, White and Green) Pepper is the dried berry/seeds of the *piper nigrum*, a plant which grows in the East and West Indies. This vine which can grow up to ten feet tall is indigenous to India and Asia. Pepper is berries that are picked about nine months after flowering. Always pick whole peppercorns over pre-ground versions. The flavor of freshly ground or cracked pepper is more robust. It is used more than any

Peppercorns were found in the nostrils of the mummy of the Pharaoh Ramsey II.

other spice around the world used to flavor all types of dishes and is an agreeable addition to many kinds of food.

Black Pepper, the spiciest, is berries that are picked unripe, dried and ground. It has a sharp, pungent aroma and flavor.

White Pepper is hotter, less subtle and mildly fermented. The berries used are ripened on the vine and soaked to make it easier to remove the outer shells. A must-have for their slight pungency.

Green Peppercorns are immature berries which are freeze-dried or packed in brine for preservation. Green Peppercorn is milder in flavor and has a fresh taste. Cayenne pepper is the powdered pod of one or more species of capsicum. The sharp taste is due to a camphor like substance found more in the pods than in the seeds.

Pepper promotes the secretion of the gastric juice. It's commonly used in stocks, pickling, and sausages. Coarsely crack Whole Peppercorns with side of a wide chef's knife and rub on to steaks and chops. Create a unique flavor depth in spice cakes, gingerbreads, and ginger cookies with a pinch of finely ground Black Pepper.

Use Black Pepper with barbecue sauces, meat marinades, and vegetable stir-fries. Sprinkle over chowders, cream soups, egg and tomato dishes. Mix with yogurt or sour cream to top a baked potato or vegetable dish. Whole Black Peppercorns can be added to stews and soups, and the liquid used to poach meat, poultry and seafood. Add the warm, delicate spicy flavor of simmered Whole Black Peppercorns to fresh fruit compotes.

History

Since the Roman times, Pepper has been the most important spice. The cities of Alexandria, Genoa, and Venice owed their economic success to Pepper. Three-thousand-year old Sanskrit literature mentions Pepper. It was one of the earliest items traded Asia and Europe. In 1101, victorious Genovese soldiers were each given two pounds of Pepper as a gift for their successful Palestinian conquest. In the Middle Ages, Europeans often used Pepper to pay rent, dowries, and taxes, and Shakespeare mentions Pepper in his plays. The need for

Pepper inspired Spanish exploration and spice trade in the 15th century. Pepper is grown in Vietnam, India, Indonesia, Malaysia and Brazil.

Poppy Seed

Poppy Seeds are tiny blue-gray seeds inside yellowish-brown capsules of opium plant indigenous to the Mediterranean. They are used to flavor breads, cakes, cookies, and rolls, in European and Middle Eastern cooking. In Turkey, they are ground to be used in desserts. In India, the ground seeds are used to thicken sauces. The seeds are also used in noodle, fish, and vegetable dishes in Jewish, German, and Slavic cooking. Poppy Seeds often used as an addition to dressings, buttered egg noodles, fruit salad, and fragrant yeast breads. Poppy Seeds add a nutty aroma and flavor and texture to breads, cakes, cookies, pastry crusts, and pancake strudels, and waffle batters.

History The Greek used the seeds as flavoring for breads in the second century, and medieval Europeans used them as a condiment with breads. Poppies are native to Mediterranean regions. Today, Holland Australia and the Czech Republic are the main producers of poppy seeds. The poppy plant was grown by the people living in Western and Central Europe between 6000 and 3500 BC. For thousands of years the plant has symbolized honor. Many cultures including Greece, Islamic and Arabic countries used the byproduct of the plant an opiate as a medicine and narcotic. In the 19th century the Opium Wars caused China to lose control of the industry.

Saffron

Saffron is the stigma of a flowering plant. Saffron, the world's most expensive spice, is costly because more than 225,000 stigmas must be handpicked to produce one pound. In its pure form, saffron is a mass of compressed, threadlike, dark burnt orange strands. These reddish strands are the most expensive with white strands coming in second. Yellow strands are of very low quality. Saffron has a spicy, pungent, and bitter flavor with a sharp and penetrating odor. A little pinch goes a long way with Saffron. Saffron is used in French bouillabaisse, Spanish paella, Milanese risotto, and many Middle Eastern dishes. Use it in Italian risottos, Spanish chicken and rice, French seafood stews and Scandinavian sweet breads.

Here are a few tips for using Saffron:

Just a pinch is enough to color and perfume sauces, soups and fish, rice and poultry dishes. Careful, though, for too much saffron imparts a medicinal taste.

Soak the threads in a bit of hot water or broth before adding them, so that the color and taste will permeate the entire dish.

Don't use wooden utensils – they are absorbent, and you don't want to waste even a tiny bit of this precious spice!

(Saffron, 2016)

History: Saffron is native to the Mediterranean and pound for pound is one of the most expensive spices sold. Today saffron is cultivated primarily in Spain. Ancient Greeks and Romans scattered Saffron to perfume public baths. The 13th century Crusaders brought Saffron from Asia to Europe, where it was used as a dye and condiment. In Asia, Saffron was a symbol of hospitality. In India, people used Saffron to mark themselves as members of a wealthy caste.

Sesame Seeds

Sesame Seed (like the seed on the bread sticks to the left) is the most commonly produced yellowish, red, or black seeds of an annual herb which grows well in hot climates. These versatile seeds have a sweet, nutty taste that complements both savory and sweet dishes. The seeds are especially flavorful and aromatic when toasted. Store them in the freezer, due to their high oil content the seeds can quickly become rancid. Sesame Seed has been enjoyed by humans since the dawn of civilization. To toast Sesame Seeds, place them in a sauce pan and stir them on medium a couple of minutes until they are lightly browned. They are used in bread products, candies, main dishes, stir-fries, or as a garnish on pasta and vegetables and Middle Eastern dishes. The Jewish and Chinese use them to make their sweets; cookie doughs, pie pastry, and breads. Sprinkle over creamed spinach, buttered noodles, eggplant dishes, and mixed vegetable stir-fries. Make a nutty spread when blended with butter or mayonnaise to be used on chicken, tuna, or turkey sandwiches.

History: Sesame Seed is probably the oldest crop grown for its taste, dating back 2000 years to China. The Egyptians used Sesame Seed as medicine around the same time. The Turks used its oil in 900 BC. The term 'open sesame' first appeared in the Arabian book "The Thousand and One Nights." The phrase refers to the seeds' ability to pop, at the slightest touch, when ripe. Sesame was imported from India to Europe during the first century. Persians used sesame oil because they had no olive oil. Africans, who called it 'benne', brought it with them to the United States in the 17th century during the slave trade. They come from Guatemala, Venezuela and Honduras.

Turmeric

Turmeric comes from the fingers which extend from the root of Curcuma longa, a leafy plant in the ginger family. The root, or rhizome, has a tough brown skin and bright orange flesh. It is boiled or steamed and then dried, and ground. Turmeric is mildly aromatic and has scents of orange or ginger. It has a pungent, bitter flavor. Turmeric is routinely added to mustard blends and relishes. Turmeric is a necessary ingredient of curry powder. It is used extensively in Indian dishes, including lentil and meat dishes, and in Southeast Asian cooking. Use Turmeric to add Eastern mystery to new favorites as well as in traditional curries, rice and chicken dishes, and condiments. Turmeric is a classic addition to chutneys, pickles, and relishes. Add a pinch of Turmeric to fish soups. Blend with melted butter and drizzle over pasta, potatoes or cooked vegetables.

History: India is the world's primary producer of Turmeric. It is also grown in Vietnam and India. Turmeric, with its brilliant yellow color, has been used as a dye, medicine, and flavoring since 600 BC. In 1280, Marco Polo described Turmeric as "a vegetable with the

> Turmeric should not be used in place of saffron because of its bitter taste.

properties of saffron, yet it is not really saffron." Indonesians used Turmeric to dye their bodies as part of their wedding ritual. Turmeric has been used medicinally throughout Asia to treat stomach and liver ailments. It also was used externally, to heal sores, and as a cosmetic.

Extracts – Vanilla, Lemon, Rose, Almond, Celery, Ginger, Cloves, Nutmeg, Strawberry, Raspberry, Pineapple & Peach

A baking essential made by soaking vanilla beans and other plants are extracted by pressure or distillation, and dissolved in alcohol. Choose the pure rather than the imitation variety, which often has additives and an unnatural flavor.

Vanilla

Vanilla is one of the most popular flavorings in the world. It is used in flavoring most desserts including: cake, candy, custard, ice cream, and pudding. Vanilla is also used to enhance the flavor of beverages and sauces. One inch of Vanilla Bean is equal to one teaspoon of Pure Vanilla Extract. Vanilla Beans should never be refrigerated because they may develop mold when chilled. They should be kept in an airtight container at room temperature. Add to desserts or beverages to boost sweet, fruity, or rich flavors. Provides smooth rich background taste - use to balance sauces for shellfish, chicken, and veal. Softens dairy flavors and reduces egginess in French toast and meringues. Add to a mug of hot chocolate, coffee, or tea for added richness.

History of Vanilla

Vanilla originated in Mexico, where the Aztecs used it to accent the flavor of chocolate drinks. The Mexican emperor, Montezuma, introduced Vanilla to the Spanish explorer Cortez, who brought it to Europe in the 16th century. The drink, made with Vanilla pods and cacao beans, became popular among the aristocracy in Europe. In 1602, a chemist for Queen Elizabeth I suggested that Vanilla could be used alone as a flavoring.

Isinglass and Gelatin

Isinglass and Gelatin are used to make jellies, and thicken soups and gravies. Isinglass is made from the intestines of fish. Its advantages over gelatin are lighter color, less flavor, and greater thickening power. In cold water it softens, swells, becomes white and opaque. In hot water it smells a little fishy. Gelatin is made from the bones of animals; it also swells in cold water, but becomes glassy and transparent, while in hot water it has somewhat the smell of glue. It is often sold for isinglass. The test of both is in the fineness and clearness of their jelly. Calves' foot jelly is delicate, but less firm. Gelatin is sold in sheets and shreds.

NOTE:

The Spices and Herbs Sections have been compiled from several works in the Public Domain and maintained by the U.S. Library of Congress. Where ever possible credit has been attributed to all sources. The photographs used in these sections are from the Public Domain, CC0 Licensing. The author took special measures to be sure that all images used meet the specification of CC0. The following is a compilation of the sources for these sections: (Goddard, 1888), (Green, 1894), (Gibbs, 1854-1909), (Medicinal Plants, 2015), (Condiments--Ginger, Whole and Ground--Specification , 1908), (Cooking school text book and House Keepers Guide, 1888) (Durkee Foodservice Website Produt & Recipe Database!, 2017) (Spices and Herbs Dictionary, 2017) (Spice and Herb Guide, 2017) (ALLSPICE (Pimenta Dioica), 2017) (Cilantro, 2017) (Food Dictionary A / B, 2017) (Mustard Seeds & Powder, 2017) (Spices, 2017) (House of Spice | Toronto, 2017) (Our Spices, 2017) (Recipe, 2017) (Our Products, 2017) (Bob's Red Mill Poppy Seeds, 2017) (Illustrated Spice Guide, 2017) (Mustard Powder, 2017)

More Food Facts!

Through-out this book there are interesting fun facts, trivia and history about the origination of our food and cooking procedures. The origin of food and cooking are as much a part of our life style and history as art, music, politics, government and religion. Technology has changed how we eat, cook and process food. The origin of eating is tied to the basis and foundation of their past.

al dente (ALDENtay) – The Italian phrase al dente means "to the tooth". Al dente means that the pasta, risotto, and vegetables is not over cooked and be chewy when eating it. The center should not be hard and the outside shouldn't be soft or over cooked. (jr, 2017)

Bagel (BAY-guhl) - Bagel derives from the Yiddish word beygl, which comes from the German word beugel meaning a "bracelet." According to legend, the world's first bagel was produced in 1683 as a tribute to Jan Sobieski, King of Poland. In the 1880s, hundreds of thousands of Eastern European Jews immigrated to America, bringing with them a love for bagels. In 1927, Polish baker Harry Lender opened the first bagel plant outside New York City in New Haven, Conn.

Baking Soda - In 1867, James A. Church began marketing sodium bicarbonate as baking soda under the Arm & Hammer label. He formed a partnership known as Church & Company

Bananas aren't grown on trees. They're part of the lily family, a cousin of the orchid, and a member of the herb family. With stalks 25 feet high, they're the largest plant on earth without a woody stem. It is the one fruit, which if left to ripen on the plant, never develops its best flavor. After they are picked, the sugar content increases from 2% to 20%. The banana is harvested green, even for local consumption.

Basil is one of the oldest herbs in the world. The ancient Greeks believed that only the king should be allowed to cut the basil plants, and he must use a sickle made of pure gold.

Herbs

Anise

The Anise seed is used whole or ground. The licorice flavor complements eggs, fruit, cheese, pastries, cakes, and cookies. The leaves are used in salads or as a garnish and dried for teas.

History: Anise grows in the wild in eastern Mediterranean and Southwest Asia. The name has no derivative and the plant is thought to aid digestion. For much of recorded history it has been cultivated. Hippocrates used it for coughs, and Pliny, the Roman scholar, used it to freshen his breath. (Photo by FotoosVanRobin; cc)

Apple Mint

Today Apple Mint is used in vinegars and as a tea.

History: The variegated varieties are sometimes known as Pineapple mint. Mint is considered a sign of hospitality.

> **Did you know?**
> Spices are more aromatic and fragrant and are usually added to sweetened food. Condiments such as pepper and mustard are pungent and are better suited to meats and food containing salt.

Basil, Cinnamon

Cinnamon Basil has a strong cinnamon scent and is popular in hot drinks and with fruits.

History: The name comes from the Greek word "basileus".

Basil, sweet

Fresh or dried basil is used in cooking to flavor French, Italian, Mediterranean, and Thai dishes. Fresh leaves are used in tomato and pesto sauces. Basil is good with veal, lamb, fish, poultry, white beans, pasta, rice, tomatoes, cheese, stews, dressings and eggs. It also is used in vinegar and as a tea.

History: Basil originated in India, where it was regarded as a sacred herb. The name comes from the Greek basileus. Basil is sensitive too cold and grows best in hot dry climates. In France Basil is known as the royal herb.

Bay Leaves

These aromatic, woodsy-tasting leaves are typically sold dried. Choose those with a rich green color. Bay Leaves are useful in hearty, home-style cooking. Add whole bay leaves to marinades, soups, stews; remove before serving. When you are making bean, chili, meat stews, spaghetti sauce, split pea soup, vegetable soup, and a Bay leaf can be added for a more pungent flavor. Alternate whole Bay Leaves with meat on skewers between seafood, and vegetables before cooking. Be sure to remove them after the meal is cooked and before you eat because they are hard to chew and may be bitter.

History: Garlands made from the bay laurel tree were used to crown the ancient Greeks and Romans victors. Laurel berry means "baccalaureate," referring to the honoring poets and scholars with garlands from the tree. Romans felt the leaves protected them against the plague and thunder. Later, the English and Italians believed that leaves warded off evil and brought good luck.

Bergamot

The leaves are used for tea and the flowers for salads or with fruit.

History: Native to North America, bergamot received its botanical name from the sixteenth century Spanish physician, Nicholas Monardez, who first discovered and described it. It was called Oswego (or Otsego) tea by early American settlers because of its use by the Oswego Indians. It was grown by the Shakers in the late 1700s in their settlement near Oswego County in New York. Today, bergamot is also known as scarlet bee balm.

Borage

Leaves can be eaten raw or sautéed like spinach. They are used in teas and to flavor wine cups. The candied stems or leaves can be used with iced beverages, cheese, fish, green salads, poultry, most vegetables, pickles, and salad dressing. The flowers are used in salads or as a garnish.

History: Borage originated in originally from Aleppo in the Middle East, but for centuries has been considered a native of Mediterranean Europe and Africa was associated with bravery. The name is from Middle English: from Old French bourrache, from medieval Latin borrago, probably from Arabic. The ancient Celtic warriors drank wine flavored with borage for give them courage. Herbalists believed that borage made people feel good and Pliny, the Roman scholar, considered Borage to be an antidepressant. The Borage's beautiful 5-pointed blue flowers were also the subjects in many examples of needlework.

Calendula

Flowers can be dried and ground and used as a good substitute for the color saffron provides in soups, stews, and poultry.

Flowers can also be used for a culinary dye in butters and custards. Avoid use during pregnancy.

History: Also known as Pot marigold, the ancient Romans named this plant after they saw it bloom the first day or "calends" of every month. For centuries, this plant was associated with the sun and believed to open with the sunrise and close with the sunset.

Caraway

The seeds are used to flavor breads, cakes, liquors, biscuits, boiled or baked onions, potato dishes, baked fruit, cream cheese, salads, sauces, soups, stews, candy, and especially in seed cakes, cookies and comfits. They also may be sprinkled into the pot when steaming turnips, beet roots, parsnips, carrots, cabbage, and cauliflower. The leaves are used in salads, soups, and stews and with spinach and zucchini. The roots can be boiled and eaten like parsnips with melted butter or white sauce.

History: Caraway Seeds were found by O'Heer in the debris of the lake habitations of Switzerland but the plant was also found in Asia Miner, India, and North Africa. Today Caraway is found all over Europe. Its properties were recognized by the ancient Egyptians and early Greeks and Romans. Popular in the Middle Ages and in Shakespeare's time. The ancient Arabs called the caraway seeds Karawya. Mixed with milk and made into bread, they are said to have formed the 'Chara' of Julius Caesar, eaten by the soldiers of Valerius.

Chamomile

The heads of the fresh flower can be used to flavor and decorate fresh salads. When dried the leaves are used in tea made with half mineral water as a beverage. There are two main types of chamomile that are used to produce the tea, German chamomile and Roman chamomile. Chamomile tea is also a digestive relaxant

History: The word "chamomile" derives, via French and Latin, from Greek word meaning "earth apple on the ground". Chamomile has been used as a traditional medicine for thousands of years to calm anxiety and settle stomachs. In the U.S., chamomile is best known as an ingredient in herbal tea.

Chervil

Fresh leaves and stems are used to flavor butter, casseroles, carrots, cheese, eggs (particularly omelets), fish, herbal butters, soups, salads, sauces, spinach, and sorrel.

History: Chervil was once called myrrh is for its volatile oil, which has an aroma like the resinous substance of myrrh. One of the traditional fines herbs in French cuisine, chervil is valued for its light parsley-like flavor with a hint of myrrh. Because it symbolizes new life it is used in a soup in Eastern Europe on Holy Thursday. Chervil's benefits were described by the seventeenth-century herbalist Nicholas Culpeper and Roman scholar Pliny believed that chervil, pleases and warms an old and cold stomach. The warmth of this herb suggested medicinal uses to many of history's herbalists. Many believe that eating the whole plant relieves hiccups.

Chive

The Strictly speaking, chives do not belong with the herbs, but their leaves are so frequently used instead of onions for flavoring salads, soups and stews. Use chive's leaves to make herbal butters and vinegars. They also may be used on grilled meats and with soft cheese. Chives is often chopped together with chervil, parsley, and tarragon to add a wonderful flavor to cooked chicken and fish, omelets, salads, steamed vegetables, and soups. Chives are used to help strengthen nails and teeth because of the calcium content.

History: Like garlic and leeks, chive belongs to the onion family, growing wild in northern Europe, Greece, and Italy. Ancient civilizations are thought to have been familiar with it, but rumors claiming that chives "send up hurtful vapors to the brain" fortunately were unfounded.

Chive, Garlic

Culinary uses include salads, soups, soft cheese, herbal butters, herbal vinegars, & grilled meats. It also attracts butterflies.

History: Also known as Chinese Chives, this herb was first recorded between 4000 and 5000 years ago in China.

Coriander

The leaves, seeds, and roots are used in cooking salsas and curries or as a garnish in salads, for seasoning soups, dressings. Coriander works well with clams, onion, oysters, potatoes, and sausage. Whole seeds are ground to be used in cheese, eggs, chili sauces, guacamole and salad dressing.

History: The popular name comes from the ancient Greek Koris, a kind of bedbug, in allusion to the disagreeable odor of the foliage and other green parts and it is commonly named cilantro. It originated in southern Europe and reached other areas centuries ago, including the hanging gardens of Babylon. Ancient Sanskrit texts, Egyptian papyrus records, and the Bible all mention coriander. The Chinese believed it imparted immortality, and it was used in love potions in the Middle Ages.

Dill

Dill is used in and. It can flavor apples, avocados, herbal butter cheese, to preserve cucumbers, cream, eggs, fish, lamb, popcorn, pork, poultry, salads, soups, sauces, and spreads vegetables, herb vinegars. **History:** In ancient times, it was grown in Palestine. Dill is native to the Mediterranean area and southern Russia. The name dill comes from the Norse dills meaning "to lull." It was once used to induce sleep. In American history, dill and fennel seed were known as "meeting".

Fennel

The licorice-flavored plant is used as garnish for fish, in sauces, soups, stews, and salads. The stock can be eaten like celery, and the tuberous roots can be boiled like a potatoe. The seeds can be used whole or ground in beverages, breads, cakes, cookies, desserts, and teas.

History: Native to the Mediterranean area, fennel was considered a magical herb that could ward off evil. It is referenced in the myths and folklore of many countries. The name is derived from the Latin foenum. Fennel grows best on limestone soils, such as the chalky lands of England and the shelly formation of Bermuda.

French Sorrel

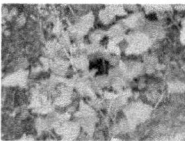

Leaves can be used in salads and soups and fish sauces or cooked like spinach. The leaves of French sorrel are almost tasteless early in the growing season, but gain acidity and flavor as the season progresses. The buck leaf sorrel has smaller angular leaves and has silvery patches on the leaves and sharp acidic flavor.

History: Commonly referred to as sorrel, and closely related to buckler leaf sorrel.

Garlic

Sautéed or fresh garlic tastes vibrant and onion like. It is added to many dishes, including spaghetti sauce, pork roast, herb butter, fresh salads, beans, stuffing, dressings, stews, soups, and marinades. The cloves are either minced or added whole and removed before the dish is served.

History: Garlic has been around for thousands of years. While its origin is unknown, some people believe it originated in Siberia, then spread to the Mediterranean area, becoming naturalized in the process. Classical writers such as Homer, Chaucer, and Shakespeare mention garlic, and it was present in the diets of early Romans, Greeks, and Egyptians.

Horehound

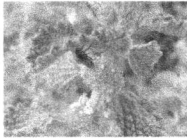

The leaves, which taste like menthol, are used in teas and candies. Often you will see this bug foraging on the plant.

History: The generic name Marrubium is derived from a Hebrew word meaning bitter. For thousands of years, horehound has been valued as a cough remedy. The Greek physician Hippocrates held this herb in high esteem for healing many ailments.

Horseradish

Horseradish root has a sharp, mustard-like taste. It is used to make a condiment and herbal butter. It is used with fish, beef, sausages, poached chicken, egg salad, potato salad, and beets.

History: Horseradish is thought to have originated in eastern Europe. In England in the 1500s, it was known as red cole and was used only for its medicinal qualities. By the 1600s it had become an acceptable condiment for fish and meat and today is part of many people's diet.

Hyssop

The mint like leaves and flowers add flavor to green salads, soups, fruit salads, and teas.

History: The name hyssop comes from the Greek *hyssopos* and the Hebrew *esob* meaning 'holy herb.' In ancient and medieval times hyssop was grown for its fancied medicinal qualities, for ornament and for cookery.

Lavender

Lavender can be used to flavor vinegars and jellies. Sometimes used as a condiment and an addition to salads and dressings.

History: Its name is derived from the Latin word "Lavo", to wash, a distillation of the flowers being anciently used in perfuming water for washing the body. Because the cultivated forms are planted in gardens worldwide, they are occasionally found growing wild as garden escapes, well beyond their natural range.

Lemon Balm

It is used in teas, beers, and wine and with fish, mushrooms, and soft cheeses. Fresh leaves are used in salads, marinades for vegetables, chicken salad, and poultry stuffing.

History: The Roman scholar Pliny and the Greek physician Dioscorides both used lemon balm as a medicinal herb. In the 1600s, it was called.

Lemon Verbena

A touch of lemon verbena can be added to fish, poultry, vegetable marinades, salad dressing, jams, puddings, and beverages. It also is used to make herbal teas.

History: There is little history or legend recorded for lemon verbena. Native to South America, the plant was found in Argentina and Chili by Spanish explorers, who brought it to Europe in the seventeenth century. There it was grown for its aromatic oil.

Lovage

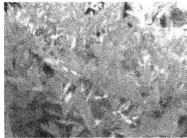

The leaves, stems, or seeds impart a celery like flavor to herbal vinegars. Fresh leaves and stems can be used in salads, and fresh or dried leaves can be added to soups. Whole or ground seeds flavor pickling brines, cheese spreads, dressings, sauces, broths, soups, stews and breads.

History: Originally from the Mediterranean area, lovage grew near the mountains of Greece and in the south of France. It was formerly used in medicine and cooking. Centuries ago lovage became established in Britain and was among the most cultivated medicinal herbs. It was grown for its roots, stems, leaves, and seeds. Today lovage is one of the lesser known herbs.

Marjoram

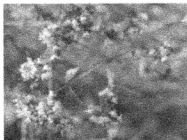

Marjoram has aromatic qualities and is a reason why it is used as a seasoning for dressings, sauces, soups, and stews. The flowers and leaves are used dried or fresh in many foods, including beef, carrots, cauliflower, eggs, fish, green vegetables, lamb, mushrooms, poultry, tomatoes and veal. It is used to flavor butter, marinades, oils, and vinegars. It is specially favored in France and Italy, but are popular also in England and America.

History: The general name origanum, meaning delight of the mountain, it is derived from two Greek words, oros meaning mountain; and ganos meaning joy; some of the species being found commonly upon mountain sides. In ancient Egypt, marjoram was used in disinfecting, healing, and preserving. Aphrodite, the goddess of love, was said to treasure this herb. The Greeks called this plant joy of the mountain and used it to make wreaths and garlands for weddings and funerals. During the Middle Ages, European ladies used marjoram in nosegays.

Oregano

Fresh or dried leaves add flavor tomato sauce, vinegar, butter, omelets, quiche, bread, marinated vegetables, beef, poultry, game, onions, black beans, and zucchini. A member of the mint family, this robust herb is commonly used in Mediterranean, South American, and Cajun cooking.

History: The name oregano is derived from the Greek word 'oros'.

Orris Root

It is used to add a bitter flavor to some liqueurs and the dried root can be chewed to freshen breath.

History: Also known as the Iris. Orris refers to the rhizome of this plant. The Iris was first cultivated commercially in Florence Italy during the middle ages.

Mint

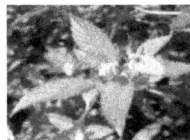

Mint flavors candy, gum, teas, mint water, vinegars, jellies, and sauces. In Europe for flavoring soups, stews and sauces for meats of unpronounced character. Among the Germans pulverized mint is commonly upon the table in cruets for dusting upon gravies and soups, especially pea and bean purees. In England and the U.S. mint is for making mint sauce, the sauce par excellence with roast spring lamb. Nothing can be simpler than to mince the tender tops and leaves very, very finely, add to vinegar and sweeten to taste.

History: The Romans crowned themselves with peppermint, and the poet Ovid referred to mint as a symbol of hospitality. The Greeks believed peppermint could clear the voice and cure hiccups. It was thought to be a remedy for mad dog bites when combined with salt. The colonists brought peppermint to America for medicinal use.

Parsley

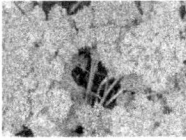

Parsley flavors sautés, grilled meat, poultry, soups, and salads. It may be used in herbal butters and vinegars or as a garnish. The Germans use both roots and tops for cooking; the former as a boiled vegetable, the latter as a potherb. In English cooking Parsley leaves are used for seasoning fricassees and dressings for mild meats, such as chicken and veal. In America we use it primarily as a garnish.

History: Herbalists in the 15th century started talking about cultivating Parsley. Parsley is thought to have originated in Sardinia, but the plant has been altered significantly by cultivation. In mythology, parsley was believed to have sprung from a Greek hero, Archemorous, the forerunner of death. Greeks crowned winners at the Isthmian games with parsley, and warriors fed the leaves to their horses.

Rosemary

Dried or fresh leaves may be used to flavor beef, cheese, eggs, fish, herbal butters, lamb, mushrooms, poultry, potatoes, stews, tomatoes, and vinegars. With an aroma of lemon and pine, this herb is used in an assortment of Mediterranean dishes. Rosemary is used for seasoning almost exclusively in Italian, French, Spanish and German cooking.

History: This aromatic plant originated in the Mediterranean area. The upright variety was valued historically for its beneficial properties and is still highly regarded today. In one legend, rosemary is used to waken Sleeping Beauty; in another, fairies take the form of snakes and lie among the rosemary. A popular saying is, "rosemary for remembrance." In ancient times, many and varied virtues were ascribed to the plant, hence its "officinalis" or medical name, perhaps also the belief that "where rosemary flourishes, the lady rules!" Pliny, Dioscorides and Galin all write about it.

Rue

Rue has a bitter taste and may be used in aromatic vinegars, beverages, marinades and sauces.

History: Sometimes referred to as the Herb-of-Grace. In historic times, it was highly reputed for seasoning and for medicine among

the Greeks and the Romans. In Pliny's time, it was considered to be effective treatment for 84 illnesses!

Sage

The herb Sage comes from an evergreen shrub in the mint family. Sages long, grayish-green leaves take on a cotton-like, velvety texture and should be ground lightly through a coarse sieve. The herb enhances duck, goose, lamb, meats, pork, and sausages. Chopped leaves flavor cheese pickles, and salads. It is one of the most popular herbs in the United States. Sage has a warm flavor and is very fragrant. The leaves should be crumbled to release its full fragrance. Because foods absorb its flavor more quickly than the whole leaf, use ground form sparingly; Sage is a great flavor enhancer for breadsticks, corn breads, muffins, and other savory breads, seafood, and vegetables. Top chicken, tuna, turkey pieces, steak, and swordfish with Sage-lemon butter. Rub cracked pepper, garlic and Sage, into pork tenderloin or pork chops before cooking.

History: The name sage, meaning wisdom, appears to have had a different origin, but as the plant was reputed to strengthen the memory, there seems to be ground for believing that those who ate the plant would be wise. Greeks and

Romans used it to cure snake bites and to invigorate the mind and body. In the Middle Ages, people drank Sage in tea and used Sage to treat colds, fevers, liver trouble, and epilepsy. Sage has become one of the world's most popular herbs. Sage is grown in the United States, Albania, Montenegro, Bosnia and Serbia.

Salad Burnet

Use for flavoring and is used in vinegars.

History: The word sanguisorba means "to drink up blood." Salad Burnet was long believed to stop hemorrhages although no modern evidence has shown this to be true.

Spearmint

Spearmint has a milder flavor than peppermint and is used in candy, gum, teas, meats, fish, vegetable dishes, fruit salad, fruit beverages, mint water, vinegars, jellies, and sauces. **History**: The Greeks believed mints could clear the voice and cure hiccups. Mints were a symbol of hospitality. Early settlers brought them to America for medicinal uses.

Summer Savory

Fresh or dried leaves flavor vinegars, herb butters, bean dishes, creamy soups, and tea. Summer Savory enhances almost any savory dish. Crush Summer Savory in your hand or with a mortar and pestle before use to release the flavor. It goes well with soups, stews, bean dishes of any sort, succotash, cabbage, and sauerkraut. Lighten up heavy stews, soups, and chowders with a garnish of Summer Savory. Top chilled, poached fish or chicken with a blend of Summer Savory, chives, lemon juice, and mayonnaise. You can also use Summer Savory for flavoring salads, dressings, gravies, and sauces used with meats such as veal, pork, duck, and goose and for Croquettes and rissoles.

History: The genus Satureja was named by the Roman scholar Pliny and is derived from the word satyr, the half-man, half-goat creature in mythology who owned the savories. Romans used Savory as an herb and seasoning even before they used pepper. They used it as a medicine, a bee sting treatment, and an aphrodisiac. When the Romans brought it to England, it was used as an ingredient in stuffing rather than as an herbal remedy. In America, it is occasionally found wild on dry, poor soils in Ohio, Illinois, and some of the western states.

Sweet Woodruff

Sweet woodruff's flowers and leaves are used for teas and to flavor wine. In Germany they add it to flavor May wine and is referred to as waldmeister meaning *master of the woods.*

History: Medieval churches prepared for religious holidays by hanging it. It was used in sachets and garlands in early England.

Tarragon

Tarragon is used to flavor asparagus, beef, broccoli, carrots, herbal butter, leeks, onions, pork, poultry, potatoes, tomatoes, mushrooms, peas, rice shellfish, and vinegars. Use fresh leaves in French dressing, salads, and tartar sauce.

History: Tarragon is a derivative of the French word "esdragon". It is native of Russia, Siberia, and Tartary for almost 1,000 years.

Thyme

Thyme flavors bread, broccoli, butter, fish, herbal, mayonnaise, mushrooms, poultry, stuffing, stews, soups, tea, and vinegars. Fresh or dried thyme may be added to salads.

This fragrant herb lends a delicate flavor to meat, poultry, and vegetables. Rub minced garlic and Thyme over beef, lamb, or pork, roasts. Season cheese, tomato, and egg dishes with Thyme. Blend fragrant Thyme into chili, pizza sauce, poultry stuffing, spaghetti or and along with any combination of basil, garlic, marjoram, oregano, sage, or rosemary. It's popular in Cajun, Creole and Mediterranean cuisines.

History: Thyme a symbol of courage and sacrifice to the Ancient Greeks. It's been said that Thyme was in the straw bed of the Christ child and the Virgin Mary. Ladies would embroider a sprig of Thyme into scarves they gave to their errant knights during the middle ages. It was also used to cure a hangover in the 18th century.

Winter Savory

Winter savory's flavor is stronger than summer savory. Fresh or dried leaves are used to flavor bean dishes, herb butters, creamy soups, tea and vinegars.

History: Roman writer Pliny named this genus "Satureja". It is derived from the word satyr, the creature in mythology who owned the savories was half-man, half-goat. The Romans used this herb for cooking and introduced it to England during Caesar's time. Portions of the Herb directory have been used. - (Dr. Michael Orzolek, 2016)

Using Fresh VS. Dehydrated Seasonings

According to Ann A. Hertzler of the Virginia Cooperative Extension Service (Hertzler, reprinted 2001), the following rules should be followed when using herbs and spices.

SEASONING SUBSTITUTIONS

FRESH OR WHOLE	DEHYDRATED
1/3 cup slices fresh onion	¼ cup onion flakes
½ teaspoon minced fresh garlic	¼ teaspoon instant minced garlic
1 clove garlic	1/8 teaspoon garlic powder
½ cup diced fresh pepper	¼ cup Bell pepper flakes
½ cup diced fresh celery	¼ cup celery flakes
½ cup diced peppers, onion, celery and carrots	¼ cup mixed vegetable flakes
½ to 1 cup fresh parsley	¼ cup instant parsley flakes
1 teaspoon chopped fresh ginger	¼ teaspoon ground ginger
1 teaspoon grated fresh lemon or orange peel.	1 teaspoon dried lemon or orange peel
	or ½ teaspoon lemon or orange extract
¼ cup chopped fresh mint	1 tablespoon dried mint
1 whole bay leaf	1 teaspoon cracked bay leaf

DRIED HERBS ½ teaspoon dried = ¼ teaspoon ground = 2 to 3 teaspoons freshly minced

Enhancing Flavors

Sweet Flavors

Instead of using sugar why not use the following spices: allspice, anise. cardamom, cinnamon. cloves, ginger, mace or nutmeg?

Savory Flavors

Seasoned salts like garlic salt contain sodium. And most sauces like steak and soy sauce are very high in sodium. Instead of using salt, sodium or fat try using the following as a substitute: basil, bay leaf, celery seed, chili powder, cumin, curry powder, dill, marjoram, mustard, oregano, paprika, pepper, rosemary, sage, tarragon, or thyme when making fondues, cheese spreads, chowder, mats, soufflés, curried dishes, beams and soups, salads, greens, tomatoes or tomato juice, pasta salads, specialty breads and rice.

Storing Spices and Herbs

Crushed or ground spices and herbs lose their potency faster than whole spices and herbs. For the best flavor and shelf life it is best to purchase the whole form and crush or grind it when cooking. When you crush the herb or spice using a mortar and pestle at the time of cooking you release the oils stored and the dish absorbs the flavor much quicker. Another way that you can crush spices and herbs is to use a rolling pin and place the spices between two pieces of cloth or by placing a small amount in between two spoons then crush it.

You should check your spices and herbs at least once per year for spoilage. You can tell that an herb or spice has lost its strength if you don't smell an aroma when it is crushed or if the color has changed (e.g. if paprika has spoiled, the color turns from red to brown.). Buying smaller quantities of spices and herbs may save you money in the long run especially if you don't use them that often.

1. Moisture damages herbs and spices. You should always store the spice or herb in a sealed container.
2. Always store your spices or herbs in a cool place away from sunlight, the stove and dishwasher. Spices like paprika, red pepper, and chili powder last longer when they are kept in the refrigerator. Sometimes I freeze sprigs of parsley and rosemary between uses.

Storage Life of Herbs and Spices

Seasoning	Storage Time
Whole	2-5 years
Ground Spices	6 months to 2 years
Leafy Herbs	3 months to 2 years
Dehydrated Vegetables	6 months

Use of Condiments

Mary E. Green, MD (Mary E. Green, 1894)**, says that:**

"Acting principally upon the nervous system through the sense of smell, condiments stimulate the flow of both the saliva and gastric juices. They materially aid digestion, and the familiar phrase, "to make the mouth water," states a physiological fact. From this standpoint, the fragrant aroma of steaming coffee and the savory odor of a stew are as truly condiments as pepper and salt; for condiments are the magic wand which transforms most commonplace of foods into essences, subtle and delicious. They are equally appropriate to the steaming potage of the French peasant and the sacrificial altars of Palestine and Greece. Nothing more closely tests the skill of the cook than his use of these appetizing flavors. Like genii of the fairy tale, they are willing, versatile and obedient as slaves; when master their pathway is strewn with sorrowful though most aromatic wrecks of soups and hors d'oeuvres. They should permeate food as incense does the atmosphere, delicate, impalpable and as indescribable as they are requisite. The too abundant use of a certain condiment or spice, the lack of another or the injudicious mingling of certain others will ruin the finest pudding, sauce or soup ever compounded."

Condiments are eaten with meat and combined with salt while spices are mainly added to articles containing sugar. Classified as follows:

Vegetable	Aromatics	Clove., cinnamon, cassia-bud, pimento or allspice, nutmeg, mace, cardamom. Pepper, cumin, coriander, fenugreek, grains of paradise, anise, dill, caraway, basil, chervil, celery, fennel, bay-leaves, summer savory, parsley, thyme, sage, sweet

| | | marjoram. Mint, tarragon, onion, leek, garlic, saffron. Capers, turmeric and curry powder. |
| | **Pungent Aromatics** | Mustard, horse-radish, ginger, chilies or cayenne pepper |

Mineral	Salt
Sauces	Chutney, tabasco, lime juice, Worcestershire, ketchup, carachi, cassareep and soy
Pickles	Various vegetables and fruis such as cucumber, olive and sanphire
Flavors	Vanilla, tonga bean, almond, chocolate, orange and various fruits
Acids	Vinegar, lime juice and verjuice
Cordials	Curacao, Noyau, Ratafia, anisette, kummel, absinthe, Chartreuse, Maraschino, etc.

Amazing Salt

0-1 Illustration by Bruce Oliver

Cruise with Bruce Food Trivia

Where does most salt come from…
underground mining or the sea?

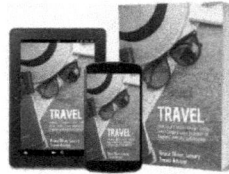

0-2 Illustration by Bruce Oliver

Different salts make a world of difference to the simplest dish.

What's wrong with regular table salt? Even though it looks very fine, it doesn't dissolve as quickly as kosher salt and has additives that give it an aftertaste.

Selected sea salts from every corner of the world offer a full palette of flavor, texture and visual appeal to any dish. Use unrefined with no artificial color or flavor added and a good salt grinder. You will be amazed at the difference in salt.

Hawaiian (Hiwa Kai) Sea Salt

This Hawaiian Sea Salt has a stunning deep black color. The salt is solar evaporated with purified black lava rock to add minerals, then combined with activated charcoal for color and to add detoxifying effects. This compliments the natural salt flavor and adds numerous health benefits to the salt. The resulting finishing salt is a very clean and yet full-flavored, ultra-pure salt that is just 84% sodium chloride, and 16% naturally occurring elements--over 80 total, including critical ocean electrolytes and trace minerals.

Peruvian Pink Salt

The source of this coarse and crunchy salt is an ancient underground ocean in Peru that feeds a spring ten thousand feet high in the Andes Mountains. Its waters seep into terraced ponds in the Sacred Valley of the Incas, where it evaporates to form salt crystals tinged pink by the ponds' flora. Hand-harvested for over two thousand years, the salt is, to this day, still transported down the mountains by burros.

Maine Sea Salt, Coarse

Snowy white and moist, this sea salt's crystals range from fine powder to coarser grains, offering a full spectrum of flavor concentration. The salt is made by evaporating seawater to 60% in pans over a Maine hard wood fire. The reduced seawater is placed in shallow pools in green houses, and solar evaporated to coarse salt crystals. The sea salt is continuously harvested in green houses and new seawater added through the summer and fall months.

Cruise with Bruce Food Trivia
Where does most salt come from... underground mining or the sea?

Salts and Sea Salts *not smelling salts*

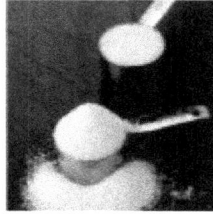

Maine Applewood Smoked Sea Salt

Produced only in very limited quantities, this sea salt is smoked over a natural apple wood fire with constant attention. The cool smoke permeates the salt and infuses the crystals with a mild but distinct slightly sweet, smoked taste. The finishing salt's medium-dense smoky flavor is perfect for meats, cheeses and salads.

Habanero Hot Salt

Solar-evaporated flake sea salt is blended with spicy hot habanero powder. Add a little or a lot to spice up that dish. Perfect for grilled fish and meats or just add as an all-purpose boost.

Australian Murray River

This exquisite salt melts on the tongue, looks like apricot colored snowflakes. Its delicate crystals melt quickly, evenly, and flavorfully, making for an ideal finishing and roasting salt.

Cruise with Bruce Trivia:

Kosher salt gets its name not because it follows the guidelines for 'kosher' foods as written in the Torah (nearly all salt is kosher, including ordinary table salt), but rather because of its use in making meats kosher, by helping to extract the blood from the meat. Rather than cubic crystals, kosher salt has a flat platelet shape. This is done in some salts by adding Yellow Prussate of Soda, (Sodium Ferrocyanate). Because kosher salt grains are larger than regular table salt grains, when meats are coated in kosher salt the salt does not dissolve readily; the salt remains on the surface of the meat longer to draw fluids out of the meat. The term kosher salt is restricted to North America, in the UK it is usually called "koshering salt", and in other parts of the world, "(coarse) cooking salt". In North America, the term 'koshering salt' has been proposed as more accurate and is sometimes used in industry (e.g. The Salt Institute), but it is rarely used in everyday language. (Salt, 2017) (Koshur Salt, 2017) (Kosher Salt, 2017) (Type of Salt and Usage, 2017)

Gourmet Salts of the Earth

0-3 Photo by Bruce Oliver - Sample Packages - Kosher Certified

Lemon Rosemary Sea Salt - This sea salt is infused with lemon, rosemary & garlic (d, 2017) for the ultimate seasoning blend that's bursting with flavor. Perfect for eggs, meat, veggies. I even use it on watermelon. ♧

Red Hawaiian Sea Salt - This salt's unique flavor is ideal for seasoning a variety of foods, especially when it comes to meat. It is widely used in Native Hawaii Dishes like the kalua pig, poke, and Hawaiian jerky. This salt also goes well with eggs, pasta, poultry, seafood, stir-fry, and grilled vegetables. (Buy Raw Alaea Hawaiian Salt, 2017)

French Grey Gourmet Sea Salt - Add incredible flavor to your entrées by seasoning with French Grey Salt. This salt is favored by the top chefs in France and all around the world.

Apple Smoked Sea Salt - This salt adds a savory and sweet smoky taste to your dishes without bitterness or harshness. For centuries pure sea salt has been smoked over an Applewood fire to produce this flavor of salt. Enjoy it on meat, seafood, salads, soups. (Smoked Applewood, 2017)

Himalayan Salt - Himalayan Salt is great for seasoning meats, a variety of egg, pasta or potato salads, soups & stews, grilled vegetables and is great for use when baking. Use for: Brine Solutions, Salt Rubs, or Sole. Also blend it with herbs to create a different type of salt. (Pink Himalayan Salt, 2017)

Order Your 5 Pak of Salts Today – Mention this book for a 10% Discount

Yes ... it's the incredible. Edible… EGG

Did you know….? IF you cover eggs
overnight with spices the eggs will carry that
taste? That's because egg shells are very
porous.

Have you ever had a BLUE egg?
My high school friend on Facebook, Elaine M., announced
that she has a breed that produces blue shelled eggs.
Did you know that there are *7-colors of eggs besides white
eggs* that chickens will lay depending upon the breed of the
chicken?
All eggs start out being white and depending upon the breed,
diet, minerals and timing in the process that the shells are
transformed to: cream, blue, green, pink, variations of solid
and speckled chocolate brown to sage colors. (Colored Eggs,
2016) - (Rainbow Eggs, 2016)

An egg is an egg ... is an egg…. Or is it?

- Every 24 to 26 hours a hen can lay an egg. Within 30
  minutes the hen begins to produce her next egg.

- There are up to seventeen thousand pores on the
  surface of an egg which allow it to absorb odors and
  flavors including other foods like onions. By storing
  them in the egg carton the eggs stay fresh longer.
  Storing them in the refrigerator, their cartons, helps
  keep them fresh up to one week longer than at room
  temperature.

- Every year in the United States 5.5 billion dozen eggs
  are laid by 240 million hens.

- White shelled eggs are produced by hens with white feathers and ear lobes. Brown shelled eggs are produced by hens with red feathers and red ear lobes.

- When you spin an egg easily it is usually hard boiled. Raw eggs wobble when you spin them.

- Some people believe that on March 21st, the Vernal Equinox and the first day of spring, an egg will stand on its small end. This may because of the date and or the properties of each egg.

- Egg yolks contain Vitamin D naturally and are one of the few foods that do.

- The diet of a hen determines the color of the yolk. When chicken farmers add the yellow-orange marigold pedals to feed the yolk takes on the color of the pedals. Addition of artificial colors is not allowed by law.

Cruise with Bruce Tip
Wrap an egg in your favorite seasoning and cheese. Let it set 48 hours then cook or use the egg. *Surprise!!!*

- Double-yoked eggs are occasionally laid by hens during their lives. Sometimes a young hen will lay an egg with absolutely no yolk, though this is abnormal.

(FAQs, 2017) (Consumers, 2017) (Trivia, 2017) (information & FAQs on Eggs, 2017) (Ch 8 - Basic Egg Facts, 2017) (Egg CAM, 2017) (Egg Facts, 2017) (National Egg Day, 2017)

Cruise with Bruce Trivia

Place one teaspoon of vinegar in with hard boiled eggs to make it easier to peel the shells off the egg after cooking.

Cruise with Bruce Family Recipes

Hotel Villa Gale – Kale Soup Cruise with Bruce Favorite - from Estoril, Portugal - Caldo Verde Soup (AKA - Green Broth Soup)

Ingredients (Serves 4 – 6 people):

1-pound tender kale or spring greens or cabbage (Couve Portuguesa), very finely shredded

Four medium floury potatoes

One small clove of garlic

2 tablespoons of olive oil

Enough water (one liter) and salt

½ small onion

½ of "Chouriço"

Preparation:

1   Cook the potatoes, smashed garlic, the chopped onion, and Chouriço in water and salt

2   Gather up the clean cabbage (Kale) leaves, free from the hardcore, and roll them up, to be able to cut an evenly with a sharp knife against a wooden or plastic board. Boil water with a little salt and after 3 minutes remove all the water and let it rest and telecoms into the soup.

3   Remove the Chouriço from the pan and cut it in slices

4   Mash the potatoes (with the garlic and onion) and return it to the broth, add the cabbage and one teaspoon of olive oil. Bring back to a boil and let it cook for just a few minutes.

5   Checked the correct seasoning, place one and two slices of Chouriço in each soup bowl, add a little olive oil, serve the soup over this and you're ready to eat.

Did you know?

- This soup originated in the Portugal's northern province of MINHO, as it reproduces the Emerald color of the countryside.
- Portuguese people are so particular that they even make soup with grass!
- Chouriço is a Portuguese term that originated in the Iberian Peninsula to describe several types of pork sausages; it is like the Spanish chorizo. Portuguese Chouriço is made with pork, fat, wine, paprika, garlic, and salt. Since Roman times the mixture has been stuffed into natural (animal intestines) or artificial casings and dried over smoke.

Slovak Dish - Gramma's Halušky a Cruise with Bruce Favorite

Ingredients (Serves 3-5 people):

> One grated potato
> One egg
> Flower to thicken mix
> Pinch of salt

Toppings

One medium onion, ½ pound butter and extra sharp cheese or cottage cheese OR Several strips of bacon along with shredded sweet cabbage OR One can of sauerkraut, one medium onion and ½ pound butter

Preparation

1. Peel and grate potato with a grater or use a blender until the mixture is soupy.
2. Combine potato, egg and flour with salt and mix together.
3. Keep adding flour in small amounts at a time to make this mixture stiff. Do so until the dough sticks to the spoon.
4. Boil water in a large pot.
5. Take one teaspoon of the mixture and drop it in the boiling water. If it falls apart add more flour to the mixture and try it again.
6. Place a small amount of the potato mixture on a large plate and flatten out with a teaspoon.
7. Chip small ¼ to ½ inch sections into the boiling water repeat this process until all of the potato mixture is gone.

8   Boil the sections until they float up to the surface (3-5 minutes). The sections will resemble a short thick noodle.
9   Drain and combine with one of the following:
10 On top of shredded sharp cheese pour onion sautéed in butter and onions.
11 Onion sautéed in butter and onions along with Cottage cheese.
12 Sweet cabbage shredded and browned with bacon fat and an onion.
13 Sauerkraut, drained and rinsed with water along with onions and butter.

NOTE: Halušky tends to be very filling. The first time you eat this dish you'll want more and will eat too much. Although it is good, try a small plate and wait a few minutes before you eat more.

Halušky (IPA: [ɦaluʃkɪ] in Czech and Slovak, singular: *haluška*; Hungarian: *galuska* or *nokedli*; Romanian: *găluşcă*; Serbian: galuška; Ukrainian: галушка; Lithuanian: *virtinukai*) are a traditional variety of thick, soft noodles or dumplings cooked in the Central and Eastern European cuisines (Slovakia, Czech Republic, Poland, Serbia, Ukraine, Romania and Hungary). Halušky can refer to the dumplings themselves, or to the complete dish. This dish is like the Spätzle the German dish.

My mom's mom was a great cook. Back then she would say a pinch of this and a pinch of that. She made ethnic dishes like "Halusky" in less than an hour.

0-1 Photo by Bruce Oliver

The first time I made the dish and told her about it, she couldn't stop laughing. "Five pounds of potatoes!", she laughed, "you could feed an army on that much food." She was right, my brothers and I invited 25 friends over to our house to eat then we brought pots of left overs to my grandmother, siblings and parents' house. We ate for a week on what we made that Saturday.

This photo was taken before my grandfather passed away in 1975 at the age of 85. He was completely blind from glaucoma by that time. Another sense that we take for granted is the ability to see. Just before he passed, he and my grandmother had an argument and all he could think of to say was: ***"And I never did like your meat loaf!"*** My grandmother roared with laughter, after 59 years, now you tell me!

Gramma's Beef Barley Soup - Cruise with Bruce

Ingredients (Serves 3-5 people):

1 Cup medium or large barley

1 shank, rib meat and neck

Water

Salt

Pepper

Garlic

Whole onions

Celery

Parsley

Carrots

1 can of tomatoes

Preparation:

1. Soak the barley in water and rinse until the water turns clear.
2. Cover the meat in water.
3. Add salt, pepper, garlic, whole onions, celery, parsley and can of tomatoes to the meat.
4. Cook the meat until it is almost done (approximately 2 to 2 ½ hours) then add barley.
5. Cook until the barley is almost done (another hour).
6. Add the diced potatoes and carrots to the pot.
7. Cook another 10 minutes or longer if the carrots are tough.

Sweet Cabbage is one of the 12 dishes that people from Eastern European countries serve for Christmas Eve.

Sweet Cabbage - Cruise with Bruce

Ingredients (Serves 3-5 people):

1 head of cabbage

½ cup of water

1-2 tablespoons of olive or cooking oil

Salt

½ onion

Flour

1-2 tablespoons of vinegar

Preparation:

1　Shred cabbage and add salt and water to saucepan then boil until tender.
2　Add cooking oil, onion, and flour to frying pan and fry until brown adding water from the cabbage pot and thicken the gravy.
3　Add vinegar to the fry pan.
4　Drain cabbage pot saving water to thin the gravy if too thick.
5　Add the gravy to the sweet cabbage pot.
6　Serve.

Potato and Cheese Pierogi - Cruise with Bruce

Ingredients (Serves 3-5 people):

1 cup of flour

1 tablespoon of salt

1 egg

Enough water to make the dough soft

Cottage cheese

Potatoes

ounces of mild to strong cheese

Preparation:

1   Mix the cottage cheese and yoke of egg (the egg white goes into the dough).
2   Mix the flour salt and egg white together with water and knead into a ball of soft dough.
3   Roll out the dough and cut into squares (should make 15 squares).
4   Boil the potatoes then drain.

5   Grate the mild to strong cheese into the potatoes and steam the potatoes until the cheese melts then mash the potatoes. Let the mixture cool.
6   Make 15 balls from the potato and cheese mixture.
7   Put one ball in the center of each of the squares and fold over the square to make get a triangle with the potato in the center. Pinch the edges of the triangle to hold the potato in.
8   Place the 15 triangles into a pot of boiling water and boil until the dough was cooked.
9   Serve the pierogi with your favorite spaghetti sauce or fry it in butter with onions covered with cheese.

Kolach Roll - Cruise with Bruce

Ingredients (Serves several people):

1 Yeast cake
1 cup of sugar
3 cups of warm milk
5 cups of flour
½ teaspoon of nutmeg
1 tablespoon of salt
2 eggs well beaten
½ soft butter

Preparation:

1 Mix yeast cake and 1 cup of sugar then put in 3 cups of warm milk. Now add 5 cups of flour and mix thoroughly.
2 Let the dough rise for 1 hour
3 Add nutmeg, salt, the two well beaten eggs, and half of the soft butter to the dough
4 Add 4 cups of flour then knead with hand.
5 Let the dough rise again after covering it with melted butter.
6 After rolling the dough out then place in pans, let it rise half an hour more

Poppy Seed Roll Filling for Kolaches:

1 c. poppy seed, ground
3/4 c. milk
Pinch of cinnamon
Pinch of cloves
1/2 tsp. salt

1 egg

3/4 c. sugar

1 tbsp. flour, mashed with butter

1/2 tsp. vanilla

Preparation:

1. Bring milk to a boil with poppy seed, cinnamon, cloves, salt and sugar. Boil about 5 minutes.
2. Add beaten egg and flour mixed with butter.
3. This makes enough filling for 2 poppy seed rolls.
4. Spread the poppy seed mixture over squares and roll into tubes.
5. Bake until bread is done.

Whole Fruit Cake - Cruise with Bruce

Ingredients:

¾ cup of sifted flour

¾ cup granular sugar

½ teaspoon baking powder

½ teaspoon salt

3 cups chopped walnuts (equal to 2 pounds of unshelled or 1 pound of shelled nuts)

1 pound pitted dates cut into pieces

1 cup of well drained maraschino cherries cut in half (1/2 cup red and ½ green)

3 eggs

1 teaspoon vanilla extract

Preparation:

1   Put the fruit and nuts into a bowl.
2   Sift dry ingredients over and mix with hands until well coated.
3   Beat eggs until foamy and add vanilla.
4   Stir eggs and vanilla into dry ingredients with spoon – well. Appears thick.
5   Spoon into tube pan or long loaf pan (9"x5"x3")
6   Bake at 300° for one hour and 45 minutes or until done.

Mom AKA Liz Oliver
Senior Editor in Chief
1927 to 2018

0-2 Photo by Bruce Oliver

Mom only made this fruit cake once per year for Christmas. Besides the Pecan Pie this was my father's favorite dessert. AT 89, she says it's time for others to make it. I've done so a couple of times but it isn't as good as when she made it. Do they leave something out when they tell you the recipe?

Now ah-days you see her more often dressed up to go out with the "Red Hat Ladies". Her group is called the SOBs (Sexy Old Broads) from Enfield. Not very politically correct, are they?

Zucchini Walnut Bread - Cruise with Bruce

Ingredients:

1 cup walnuts

4 eggs

2 cups of granular sugar

1 cup of vegetable oil

2 cups of grated zucchini (with skin)

1 cup of raisins

1 teaspoon of vanilla

½ cups of un-sifted. Unbleached all-purpose flour

1 ½ teaspoons of baking soda

1 ½ teaspoon of salt

1 teaspoon cinnamon

3 teaspoons baking powder

Preparation:

1   Chop walnuts into medium size pieces
2   Beat eggs gradually beating in sugar then oil
3   Combine dry ingredients and add to first mixture alternating with zucchini
4   Stir in raisins, walnuts and vanilla.
5   Turn into 2 greased and lightly floured loaf pans (9"x5"x2 ¾")
6   Bake on lowest rack at 350°for approximately 55 minutes or until loaf tests done
7   Let stand for 10 minutes then turn onto wire racks
8   If desired, sprinkle with confectionary sugar
9   Loafs freeze well

Oliver Family Birthday Cake - Cruise with Bruce

Ingredients:

2 cups of sugar

4 eggs

1 cup of whole milk

½ teaspoon almond extract

2 cups of flour

2 teaspoons of baking powder

Preparation:

1   Put eggs over sugar then beat for 12 minutes
2   Heat milk to boiling point adding almond extract
3   Cool the milk
4   Sift flour once, 2nd time add baking powder to flour
5   Add flour to egg mixture and mix
6   Add warm milk slowly and beat
7   Split batter between two 10" cake pans and bake for approximately 30 minutes at 350°.

0-3 Photo via Bruce Oliver

> **NOTE**: This recipe also makes 3 dozen cupcakes 25 minutes at 350° OR 1 dozen cupcakes (bake for 25 minutes at 350° plus one tube cake (bake for 30 minutes at 350°)

Boiled Milk Icing - Cruise with Bruce

Ingredients:

1 cup of granular sugar
¼ pound of butter
½ cup of Crisco
Pinch of salt
1 teaspoon of almond or vanilla
1 cup milk
1 tablespoon flour

Preparation:

1   Boil milk and flour stirring constantly so it doesn't burn.
2   Add the balance of ingredients and heat together.
3   When the ingredients dissolve and thicken take off the heat.
4   Let the mixture cool and spread over the cake.

Bob's Swedish Apple Pie - Cruise with Bruce

Robert Allen Oliver, 1963-1999

0-4 Photo by Bruce Oliver

My brother Bob loved to make this recipe and this is a tribute to him.

This picture was taken of him while we traveled in England. He graduated from culinary school and loved to cook. He went on to join the military where he spent over ten years in service and reached the rank of Sargent. He passed away several years ago and is missed by all who knew him.

God bless him and all who serve and served in the military.

Ingredients:

1 teaspoon cinnamon

1 tablespoon sugar

Five apples – sliced

Pour first two ingredients over the sliced apples

1 cup of sugar

1/4 stick of melted butter

1 egg

1 cup of flour

Pinch of salt

½ cup of chopped nuts

Preparation:

1   Mix alone.
2   Put apples, cinnamon and sugar into a pie plate.
3   Spread above mixture over the sliced apples, cinnamon and sugar.
4   Bake at 400° for 10 minutes then 350° for 50 minutes.

Streusel Coffeecake - Cruise with Bruce

Ingredients:

¾ cup of sugar

1/3 cup of Crisco oil

1 egg

½ cup of milk

1 ½ cups of sifted regular flour

2 teaspoons double-acting baking powder

½ teaspoon salt

Streusel Topping Ingredients and Preparation

½ cup of light brown sugar

2 tablespoons of regular flour

2 teaspoons of cinnamon

2 tablespoons of Crisco oil

½ cup of finely-chopped walnuts

Combine all ingredients with a fork. Sprinkle Streusel
Topping on batter per instructions below

Preparation:

1. Combine sugar, Crisco oil, and egg.
2. Add milk and beat thoroughly.
3. Stir in combined dry ingredients.
4. Beat until smooth.
5. Spread in a greased 9" square pan.
6. Sprinkle with Streusel Topping.
7. Bake at 375° for 30-35 minutes.

Sour Cream Coffee Cake - Cruise with Bruce

Ingredients:

¼ pound of butter

1 cup of sugar

2 eggs

1 cup of sour cream

1 teaspoon of vanilla

2 cups of flour

1 teaspoon baking powder

1 teaspoon soda

¼ teaspoon salt

Preparation:

1   Cream butter adding sugar and eggs and beat.
2   Add sour cream and vanilla.
3   Add sifted dry ingredients.
4   Put half of the batter in a greased tube pan.
5   Sprinkle with ¾ of the topping.
6   Add the rest of the batter and topping.

Topping:

¼ cup of sugar

1 teaspoon of cinnamon

1 cup of chopped nuts

Ingredients:

1 cup of flour

¼ cup of sugar

2 teaspoons of baking powder

½ teaspoon of salt

¾ cup of regular Ralston Cereal (1 cup if it's instant)

1 cup of milk

Preparation:

1. In a bowl add flour, sugar, salt, baking powder, and milk – mix together to blend everything together.
2. In another bowl beat egg, add ¼ cup of oil, blend and add 1 cup of water.
3. Then add egg, oil and water to the first bowl and blend until all is moistened.
4. Grease muffin tins and fill ¾ full – makes 12 Ruffins.
5. Bake at 400° for 20 minutes.

Aunt Ann

0-5 Photo by Bruce Oliver

My Godmother, Aunt Ann was famous for the muffins that she cooked all the way to the ripe age of 96. Not long after this photo was taken, she passed away just 10 days short of one year after my uncle. She's probably making these muffins where ever she is.

Spero's Spaghetti Sauce - Cruise with Bruce

Ingredients:

½ pound hamburg

¼ cup butter

2 chopped onions

4 cloves of garlic

Cinnamon

Salt

Pepper

Allspice

Preparation:

1   Place hamburg in frying pan and fry until all the water and fat is removed.
2   In another pan fry butter, onions, garlic, then sprinkle cinnamon, salt pepper and allspice.
3   When browned put in tomato paste and cook for 10-12 minutes until red.
4   Put in hamburg, etc.
5   Cook all 10-12 minute more.
6   Put hot water into frying pan and then into mix.

7   Cook slowly at least ½ hour then raise heat until thick.

Bibliography

(n.d.). Retrieved from
   http://www.spiceadvice.com/newsa/usage/chart.html
10 Incredible Facts Sense of Smell. (2014). Retrieved from
   Everyday Health:
   http://www.everydayhealth.com/news/incredible-
   facts-about-your-sense-smell/
(1888). In J. Corson, *Cooking school text book and House
   Keepers Guide* (pp. 13-16). New York City: Orange
   Judd Company.
(1908). In *Condiments--Ginger, Whole and Ground--
   Specification* .
20 Facts Sense Smell. (2016). Retrieved from UK Mirror
   Lifestyle Magazine:
   http://www.mirror.co.uk/lifestyle/health/20-
   fascinating-facts-sense-smell-1977351
(2016). Retrieved from Sharpe Hill Vineyard, Pomfret, CT:
   http://sharpehill.com
(2016). Retrieved from Chateau Souverain, Sonoma County
   (California): http://www.souverain.com
ACH FOOD COMPANIES, I. -C. (2016). *Spice Advice -
   Spice Usage Tips*. Retrieved from
   http://www.spiceadvice.com/newsa/usage/chart.html
Adastra Winery. (2016). Retrieved from
   http://www.adastrawines.com/
Adirondack Winery. (2016). Retrieved from
   http://www.adirondackwinery.com
All Spice. (n.d.). Retrieved from http://Allspice.com
ALLSPICE (Pimenta Dioica). (2017). Retrieved from
   http://www.cookbook.hu:
   http://www.cookbook.hu/angol_receptek/allspice.ht
   ml
Artezin Wines. (2016). Retrieved from
   http://www.artezinwines.com/
Bailyn, L. (2006). *Breaking the Mold: Redesigning Work for
   Productive and Satisfying Lives*. Ithaca: ILr Press -
   Cornell University Press.

Baiting Hollow Farm Vinyard (Calverton, NY). (n.d.).
Retrieved from
http://www.baitinghollowfarmvineyard.com

Beringer. (2016). Retrieved from
http://www.beringer.com/knights-valley

Billsboro Winery (Geneva, NY). (2016). Retrieved from
www.billsborowinery.com

Bob's Red Mill Poppy Seeds. (2017). Retrieved from
iherb.com: https://www.iherb.com/Bob-s-Red-Mill-
Poppy-Seeds-8-oz-226-g/29594

Brotherhood Winery (Washingtonville, NY). (2016).
Retrieved from http://www.brotherhood-winery.com

Brotherhood Winery, (Washingtonville, NY). (2016).
Retrieved from http://www.brotherhood-winery.com

Buy Raw Alaea Hawaiian Salt. (2017). Retrieved from Z
Natural Foods:
https://www.znaturalfoods.com/alaea-hawaiian-salt-
fine

Ch 8 - Basic Egg Facts. (2017). Retrieved from
https://afs.ca.uky.edu: https://afs.ca.uky.edu/files/8-
basic_egg_facts.pdf

Chateau Ste Michelle (Woodinville, WA). (2016). Retrieved
from https://www.ste-michelle.com

Cilantro. (2017). Retrieved from epicurus.com:
https://www.epicurus.com/food/cilantro/

Clinton Vineyards. (2016). Retrieved from
http://www.clintonvineyards.com

Colored Eggs. (2016). Retrieved from
http://www.hobbyfarms.com/7-chickens-to-raise-
for-colorful-eggs-3/

Consumers. (2017). Retrieved from Cal Maine Foods:
http://calmainefoods.com/consumers/

Cruise with Bruce Show - Ryan talks travel. (2011).
Retrieved from
http://www.blogtalkradio.com/cruisewithbruce/2011
/06/22/ryan-oreilly-heir-to-the-oreilly-auto-parts-
talks-travel

Cruise with Bruce Show interview Boston Harbor Cruise.
(2011). Retrieved from

http://www.blogtalkradio.com/cruisewithbruce/2011
/08/09/rags-to-riches-story-richard-oleary-spirit-of-
boston-cruise

*Cruise with Bruce Show with Rick Robinson's interview on
Ireland and his book Manifest Destiny.* (2011).
Retrieved from
http://www.blogtalkradio.com/cruisewithbruce/2011
/03/30/rick-robinson-ireland-on-cruise-with-bruce-
rick-robinson-talks-ireland-n-manifest-destiny

Cruise with Bruce YouTube Channel. (2014). Retrieved from
https://www.youtube.com/watch?v=lqQnqKxIgbQ

Cullari Vineyards and Winery (Hershey, PA),. (2016).
Retrieved from http://www.cullarivineyards.com

d. (2017). Retrieved from San Francisco Salt Co:
https://wine.woot.com/offers/san-francisco-salt-co-
sampler-6-7

Der Pollerhof (Weinviertel, Austria). (2016). Retrieved from
http://www.pollerhof.at/english-/index.html

Domaine Pierre Luneau-Papin. (2016). Retrieved from
http://www.domaineluneaupapin.com

Dr. Frank's Vinifera Wine Cellars. (2016). Retrieved from
http://www.drfrankwines.com

Dr. Michael Orzolek, P. o. (2016, N/A N/A). *Herb
Directory.* (Penn State University) Retrieved from
Penn State » Extension » Plants and Pests » Home
Lawn and Garden » Herbs:
http://extension.psu.edu/plants/gardening/herbs

Durkee Foodservice Website Produt & Recipe Database!
(2017). Retrieved from http://www.spiceadvice.com:
http://www.spiceadvice.com/encyclopedia/Mustard_
Seed.html

Egg CAM. (2017). Retrieved from https://lancaster.unl.edu:
https://lancaster.unl.edu/4h/embryology/games/Who
Chick.htm

Egg Facts. (2017). Retrieved from Opal Foods:
http://www.opal-foods.com/egg-facts.html

Ellen Galinski, P. (2014, February 1). *Overwork in America:
When the Way We Work Becomes Too Much.*
Retrieved from Families and Work Institute:

http://www.familiesandwork.org/overwork-in-america-when-the-way-we-work-becomes-too-much/

FAQs. (2017). Retrieved from Dutch Farms: http://dutchfarms.com/contact/faq/

Fontana Candida Vineyards, Lazio, Italy. (2016).

Food Dictionary A / B. (2017). Retrieved from What's Cooking America: https://whatscookingamerica.net/Glossary/A.htm

Foodterms. (2016). Retrieved from http://www.foodterms.com/encyclopedia/celery-root/index.html?oc=linkback

Gibbs, W. M. (1854-1909). Spices. In W. M. Gibbs, *Spices and how to know them* (pp. 7-178). Buffalo, N.Y.: The Matthews-Northrup Works.

Girard Napa Valley. (2016). Retrieved from http://www.girardwinery.com

Goddard, F. B. (1888). Spices and Herbs. In F. B. Goddard, *Grocers' Goods: A Family Guide to the Purchase of Flour, Sugar, Tea, Coffee, Spices, Canned Goods, Cigars, Wines, and All Other Articles Usually Found in American Grocery Stores* (pp. 16,39-42,47). New York City: The Tradesmen's Publishing Company.

Green, M. E. (1894). In M. E. Green, *Condiments, spices and flavors*. Chicago: The Library of Congress.

Gump, B. B., & Matthews, K. A. (2000). In B. B. Gump, & K. A. Matthews, *Are Vacations Good for Your Health? The 9-Year Mortality Experience After the Multiple Risk Factor Intervention Trial* (pp. September/October 2000 - Volume 62 - Issue 5 - pp 608-612). American Psychosomatic Society.

Hayne Vineyard. (2016). Retrieved from http://www.chasecellars.com/hayne-vineyard/

Henry of Pelham Estate Winery, ON Canada. (2016). Retrieved from http://henryofpelham.com/

Hertzler, A. A. (Reprinted 2001). Herbs and Spices. *Publication 348-907*.

Holland America Line Interview. (2011). Retrieved from http://www.blogtalkradio.com/cruisewithbruce/2011

/05/04/holland-america-line-cruise-with-bruce-radios-cruise-news

House of Spice | Toronto. (2017). Retrieved from ehouseofspice.com: http://www.ehouseofspice.com/index.php%3Fview%3Dcurry-lovers-spice-collection

Illustrated Spice Guide. (2017). Retrieved from ruchiskitchen.com: http://www.ruchiskitchen.com/illustrated-spice-guide/

information & FAQs on Eggs. (2017). Retrieved from Egg Chicken Anatomy: https://animalcorner.co.uk/chicken-eggs/

Jazz musician Chris Geith Cruise with Bruce as we talk about his boyhood home and favorite vacations to Lake Como. (2011). Retrieved from http://www.blogtalkradio.com/cruisewithbruce/2011/02/23/chris-geith-music-on-cruise-with-bruce-chris-geith-talks-milan-italy-weather-channel-jazz-music

Jonathan Edwards Winery. (2016). Retrieved from www.jedwardswinery.com

Jonathan Edwards Winery, Stonington, CT. (2016). Retrieved from www.jedwardswinery.com

jr, C. F. (2017). *Starch Cookery.* Retrieved from Information on Starch Cookery: https://www.scribd.com/document/342784572/Starch-Cookery

Kosher Salt. (2017). Retrieved from Appropedia: http://www.appropedia.org/Kosher_salt

Koshur Salt. (2017). Retrieved from Bulk Barn: http://www.bulkbarn.ca/en/Products/All/Kosher-Salt-320

LaBelle Winery (Amherst, NH) . (2016). Retrieved from http://www.labellewinerynh.com

Marenco Vini Winery. (2016). Retrieved from Marenco Vini Winery: http://en.marencovini.com/

Marimar Estate Don Miguel Vineyard (Sebastopol, CA). (2016). Retrieved from http://marimarestate.com/don-miguel-vineyard

Marques de Caceres. (2016). Retrieved from
    http://www.marquesdecaceres.com/?lang=en

Mary E. Green, M. (1894). *Condiments, Spices and Flavors.*
    Library of Congress.

Masciarelli Winery. (2016).

Medicinal Plants. (2015, 11 23). Retrieved from Library of
    Congress - Science Reference Services:
    https://www.loc.gov/rr/scitech/tracer-
    bullets/medicplantstb.html

Michele Chiarlo Nivole. (2016).

Middle Ridge Winery. (2016). Retrieved from
    http://www.middleridge.com

Mitchum, L. (2014, 12 8). Press Officer. *The London Eye
    AKA EDF Energy London Eye & The Millennium
    Wheel | Bruce Oliver*. (B. Oliver, Interviewer)
    Cruise with Bruce Radio Show. Retrieved from
    http://www.blogtalkradio.com/cruisewithbruce/2014
    /12/08/the-london-eye-aka-edf-energy-london-eye-
    the-millennium-wheel-bruce-oliver-1

Mount Palomar. (2016). Retrieved from
    http://www.mountpalomarwinery.com

Mount Palomar Vineyard. (2016). Retrieved from
    http://www.mountpalomarwinery.com

Mount Palomar Winery. (2016). Retrieved from
    http://www.mountpalomarwinery.com

Mustard Powder. (2017). Retrieved from dir.indiamart.com:
    https://dir.indiamart.com/navi-mumbai/mustard-
    powder.html

Mustard Seeds & Powder. (2017). Retrieved from
    dmlgroup.com:
    http://dmlgroup.in/?portfolio_page=mustard-seeds-
    powder-yellow-black

NASA Earth Observatory. (2014). Retrieved from
    http://earthobservatory.nasa.gov/IOTD/view.php?id
    =85900

National Egg Day. (2017). Retrieved from One You:
    https://www.oneyoucheshireeast.org/national-egg-
    day/

Ordering Wine. (2014). Retrieved from
http://www.businessinsider.com/what-not-to-do-
when-ordering-wine-2013-12

Otter Cove and Oh Wines - Monteray, CA. (2016). Retrieved
from www.ottercovewines.com

Our Products. (2017). Retrieved from
blackbuggybulkfoods.com:
http://www.blackbuggybulkfoods.com/products.php

Our Spices. (2017). Retrieved from Olde Thompson:
https://www.oldethompson.com/our_spices.aspx

Paradise Hills Winery (Wallingford, CT). (2016). Retrieved
from http://paradisehillsvineyard.com/wine-menu/

Paradise Hills Winery (Wallingford, CT). (2016). Retrieved
from http://paradisehillsvineyard.com/wine-menu/

Paradise Hills Winery, Wallingford, CT. (2016). Retrieved
from http://paradisehillsvineyard.com/

Pellegrini Vineyards, Cutchogue, NY. (2016). Retrieved
from http://pellegrinivineyards.com

Photo by FotoosVanRobin; cc. (n.d.).

Pink Himalayan Salt. (2017). Retrieved from Anisas Secrets:
http://www.anisassecretsspices.com/store/store/
anisas-secrets-gourmet-salts/sherpa-pink-himalayan-
salt-8-oz/

Premier Cru Vineyard. (n.d.). Retrieved from
http://www.billaud-simon.com/en/

Premier Cru Vineyard. (2016). Retrieved from
http://www.billaud-simon.com/en/

Radio Show. (2014). Retrieved from
http://www.blogtalkradio.com/cruisewithbruce/2014
/12/12/history-of-cliveden-house--waldorf-astor-
estate-taplow-birkshire-uk-england

Rainbow Eggs. (2016). Retrieved from
http://www.fresheggsdaily.com/2012/02/rainbow-of-
egg-colors.html

Recipe. (2017). Retrieved from senteursdangkor.com:
http://www.senteursdangkor.com/html/en/our_recipe
.php

Robert Mondavi Winery. (2016). Retrieved from
http://www.robertmondaviwinery.com

Saffron. (2016). Retrieved from
http://espacepourlavie.ca/en/saffron

Salt. (2017). Retrieved from Cooking Wiki:
https://www.cookipedia.co.uk/recipes_wiki/Salt

Saracco Winery's. (2016). Retrieved from
http://www.paolosaracco.it/en/

Sense of Smell. (2013). Retrieved from
http://www.ncbi.nlm.nih.gov/pubmedhealth/PMHT0
025081/

Sense of Taste. (2012). Retrieved from
http://www.ncbi.nlm.nih.gov/pubmedhealth/PMH00
72592/

Sharpe Hill Vineyard (Pomfret, CT). (2016). Retrieved from
http://sharpehill.com

Simon, B. (2016). Retrieved from http://www.thekitchn.com

Smoked Applewood. (2017). Retrieved from San Francisco
Salt Co: https://www.sfsalt.com/smoked-applewood-
sea-salt-fine-grain

Spice and Herb Guide. (2017). Retrieved from
Neareast.com: http://www.neareast.com/cooking-
concepts/herb-and-spice-guide

Spices. (2017). Retrieved from masalatize.com:
http://www.masalatize.com/spices/

Spices and Herbs Dictionary. (2017). Retrieved from Italian
Cook: http://www.italiancook.ca/spice-herb.htm

Summers Winery, Calistoga, CA. (2016). Retrieved from
https://www.summerswinery.com

Taylor Brooke Winery. (2016). Retrieved from
http://taylorbrookwinery.com

Trivia. (2017). Retrieved from Egg Tester:
http://www.eggtester.com/trivia

Type of Salt and Usage. (2017). Retrieved from Messianic
Torah Truth Seeker: http://www.messianic-torah-
truth-seeker.org/Torah/Kashrut/ Salt-Varies-
Usage.html

Willamette Valley Vineyards. (2016). Retrieved from
http://wvv.com

Windsor Vineyards (Healdsburg, CA). (2016). Retrieved
from http://www.windsorvineyards.com

Interactive Resources

Website: http://www.BruceLuxuryTravel.com
Blog   : http://LuxuryTravelAdviserPodcast.com
Quarterly Sweepstakes: http://Win.CruiseWithBruce.com
Contact: http://VirtualLuxury.net/contact
Facebook:
      http://www.facebook.com/cruiseradionetwork
      http://www.facebook.com/cruisewithbruce
      http://www.facebook.com/groups/BruceOliverTV
Twitter: http://www.twitter.com/BruceOliverCT
YouTube: http://www.youtube.com/cruisewithbruce
Blog Talk Radio:
http://www.blogtalkradio.com/cruisewithbruce/podcast
iTunes: https://itunes.apple.com/us/podcast/food-wine-art-theme-based/id400027948?mt=2
TuneIn Radio:
http://tunein.com/radio/Cruise-with-Bruce-p382915/
Instagram: https://instagram.com/bruceoliverct/
Pinterest: https://www.pinterest.com/cruisewithbruce/
Scratch and Sniff Travel™
      http://ScratchAndSniffTravel.com
Bruce Oliver, Scent-sational Traveler™
      http://scentsationaltraveler.com/
Scent-Sational Travel™ Books
      http://ScentsationalTravelBooks.com
Promotions   http://Promotions.CruiseWithBruce.com
Yelp   https://www.yelp.com/biz/virtual-luxury-network-cruise-with-bruce-enterprises-greenwich
Bruce Oliver TV: http://BruceOliverTV
Smart TV Network: http://SmartTVtraveler.com
Travel Coloring Books: http://TravelingColoringBooks.com

Index

Win Sweepstakes

Scan the QR Code above to enter Signature Travel Network's Quarterly Sweepstakes.

    http://Win.CruiseWithBruce.com

Every quarter we award an all-inclusive vacation to one lucky winner.

Scan the QR Code above to get a quarterly subscription to a 68-page Travel Magazine

    http://Win.CruiseWithBruce.com

Enter all of the information that is requested and be sure to click on email notifications.

About Bruce Oliver – *This book is an introduction to the Scratch and Sniff Travel Series and the Traveling Coloring Books.*

Bruce Oliver, native of Enfield, CT spends winters in Orlando or Las Vegas. He has traveled to over 49 states, 56 countries and 6 continents. Bruce's paternal great grandparents immigrated to the U.S. from the London (Enfield) England in the 1800's to settle on the country road that is now known as Oliver Road, Enfield, Connecticut. His paternal great grandparents are also from Italy. His maternal grandfather walked from his home near Prague when he was nine years old to take a boat to America from Great Britain. Quite a feat for a nine-year old.

Bruce has a passion for global travel and photography.

He's the recipient of the Travel Weekly Silver Magellan Award for individuals in the travel industry and was awarded the 2014 Best of Enfield Cruise Agents. He's a member of OASIS Agent and the Signature Travel Network.

Bruce has certification with the Cruise Line Industry Association (CLIA) and has credentials from the International Air Transport Association (IATA). He is a Luxury Travel Specialist and has "destination specialist" certifications from all over the world as well as a close working relationship with most the cruise lines and travel operators. He is a Level 2 Member of the United Nations Educational, Scientific, and Cultural Organization (AKA - UNESCO): World Heritage Convention.

He also has **travel photographer** press credentials from the **National Press Association** and the **ITWPA**. He is a Professional Photographer registered with the International VR Photography Association (IVRPA) specializing in 360°

Virtual Tours. He's listed as a **Charter Member of the Library of Congress** and the **Microsoft Alumni Association**.

He's the recipient of many honors and awards in his community and higher education. In 1989, he graduated with an MBA from the University of Hartford. Bruce is listed in **MARQUIS: Who's Who in America, Who's Who in the World** and **Who's Who in American Education**. In 2019, Bruce was recognized by **Albert Nelson Marquis with the Lifetime Achievement Award** after being listed as a biographical reference in 68 diverse publications. Bruce has been a member of the National Eagle Scouts Association since 1967 and is a Vigil Honor Member in BSA's: Order of the Arrow. While attending high school, he was awarded the DeKalb Agricultural Accomplishment Award and the Connecticut State Farmer Degree from the Future Farmers of America.

If you like this transcript please write a review by going to:
http://Amazon.com/author/bruceoliver/

You can listen to my podcasts by going to:
http://alpha.podcasttoradio.com/15609

www.ingramcontent.com/pod-product-compliance
Lightning Source LLC
Chambersburg PA
CBHW061148040426
42445CB00013B/1614